Good wishes

V. Sood

INDIA
THE
FIRST WORLD
CULTURAL COUNTRY

INDIA
THE
FIRST WORLD
CULTURAL COUNTRY

V. Sood

Oscar's Institute of Art and Research

First Published in India in 2014 by
Oscar's Institute of Art and Research
S.C.O. 85, Sector-5, Panchkula-134109 (Haryana)
India
email : indiathefirstworldcountry@gmail.com

ISBN 978-93-5156-985-5

Delhi Branch
J-102, South Extension, Part-I
New Delhi-110049
India

Canada Branch
10 Ron Rose Road
Vaugn, Ontario
L4K5W5
Canada

A large amount from the proceeds of the sale of this book will be used for the
Clean and Green For My Child
Campaign in India

For online purchase of this book contact
www.oscarartandresearch.com

Price
₹ 495.00
US$ 24.95

Designed by
Arya Graphics, Gandhidham, Gujarat, India

Printed and bound at
Ramesh Pustak Bandhnalya, Kailash Nagar, Delhi

To my childhood friend

Late Mr. C. K. Maini

He was one of the most intelligent and caring person I have ever known also he was one of the first graduates of IIM Kolkata

He cared for India and motivated me in writing this book

Preface

This book is about comparing Indian culture with the American culture. Culture has been defined as the way of living of people of a country which has been compared in this book. In order to effectively conclude, I went to India twice, in the last three years.

Earlier, I heard lot of negativism about India for many years, so I went there after 13 years from Canada to find out the facts. I have been living in Canada since 1971 and was educated in USA.

I travelled to about 15 cities, big and small like Delhi, Mumbai, Banglore, Amritsar, Ludhiana, Karnal, Meirut, Ahmdabad, Surat, etc. by car, train and by air. I stayed with friends, family members and in hotels, during my two trips of about five months in December 2011 and December 2012.

I noticed a lot of care and interaction among people during my visits to a hospital to see my childhood friend, noticed the same among family members and friends while visiting them.

I also noticed parents spending their valuable time teaching their children. Educating them is their top priority. Rich and the poor are equally dedicated to the children's education. Comparing with School Boards of

America and India, I found out that 3rd grade students in India learn the same subject and material as a 6th grade students in America. On top of it, general knowledge is taught to the students from the Grade 1 in India. Parents are willing to sacrifice their most valuables to give education to their children. The same dedication is lacking in America.

I noticed vast majority of elderly live with the families in India, giving company to grand children, playing with them, giving them education and sharing their valuable experiences. This makes older people feel happier and healthier. In America, most of the older people live in the nursing homes or live alone in their homes.

In India, well being is defined by the growth of other people's lives, caring for their families. This is done collectively, a tendancy naturally prevalent in Indian society.

In America, families do not get mentioned. Well being is defined by individualism.

Today, average Indian is richer than average American. In recent days, we have seen foreclosure of the properties of millions of people all over USA, losing equities by more than 50%. During the same period, properties in India increased 2-3 times, making Indians, richer. Even the slum houses in Mumbai are worth more than $40,000. There is no financing on about 90% of the homes in India while in America it is reverse. This was the reason of mass foreclosure in America during last few years. There is more gold with Indian people and the saving rate is 2-3 times higher than that of the Americans.

Yoga and meditation started in India many years ago. Medical treatment of a lot of diseases which are not cured by regular medicines, is being achieved by yoga exercises and meditation. It is also getting very popular in America.

Father of the Nation, Mahatma Gandhi, brought independence to India. He taught the Nation to live peacefully and further emphasized for self-sufficiency (Swadeshi). India is the world's largest democracy. Today India, produces all kinds of cars, even electric car called Reva. There are large petroleum, heavy and other industries in India.

Taj Mahal, one of the most beautiful monuments of the world, is a cultural symbol of India. It was built in memory of Mumtaz by the King Shah Jahan.

More than 50% of the American marriages end up in divorce, causing huge problems for the children. In India, the divorce rate is less than 2%. About 50% children are from the divorced parents in America.

53% children are born to unmarried women in America (as per New York Times). In India it is less than 1% and is socially not acceptable.

According to the UN Report (2010), for each 100,000 population, America has 28 rapes compare to 2 in India. A girl was gang raped during a class in Elmont, New York (February 2012) while her teacher sat there and did nothing. According to New York times, rapes in New York city are three times more than those in Mumbai.

Guns are a big problem in USA. Recently, the ex-Deputy Prime Minister of Australia, Tim Fischer, spoke on CNN and discouraged tourists to visit America as 80 people are shot and killed everyday by the guns there.

Drugs are very common in America. Many celebrities, including Michael Jackson and Whitney Houston, died of drugs overdose. Drugs overdose kills nearly 120 persons in America every day.

In the last few years, many politicians have been jailed for corruption in USA. In one state, Illinois, 4 Governors have been sent to Jail. There are about 3,000,000 people in jails of USA. In India, the corruption is wide spread and there are about 350,000 people in jails.

In 1986, a well known Wall Street Icon, Ivon Boesky, said in a speech that "greed is healthy". Hundreds of people have been convicted in USA for fraud and inside trading. Even many companies including, Johnson and Johnson, has paid billions of dollars in fines for corruption.

In 2010, there were more than 700,000 cars stolen in America. Store thefts cost US retailers, $40 billion (Rs. 2,40,000 Crores) in 2010.

In 2012, over 50 charities in America spent less than 3% of the donations on the needy, balance of the money was swallowed in fees and for personal benefits of the officials of the charities. Some of the CEO's of these Charities earn nearly one million dollars a year including the benefits.

One million Americans go bankrupt every year because of health related costs. Many health related professional, including doctors, pharmacist have recently been jailed for corruption.

Inspite of this we should not overlook the shortcomings prevelant in India. India can learn many things from America. American people are very hardworking, responsible and punctual. The other strong point of America is cleanliness and hygienic consciousness.

Though the USA is the biggest polluter of the world yet its surroundings are cleaner and more hygienic than those in India. India needs cleaning in large scale as well as to pay attention to hygienic values. Major work is required in this field and in the traffic control.

According to Edward Taylor and Swami Vivekananda, culture is the characteristic way of life, inspired by the fundamental of life, according to which people live. Culture is not the material thing.

Thus the culture of India is far superior to that of America.

—V. Sood

Contents

Contents

What is Culture

Edward B. Taylor

The term was first used in this way by the Pioneer English Anthropologist, Edward B.Taylor in his book, "Primitive Culture," published in 1871. Taylor said, "the Culture is knowledge, that complex whole which includes belief, art, law, custom and any other capabilities and habits by man as member of society. Culture is a powerful human tool for survival, it is fragile as it only exists on our minds and constantly changing. Man made buildings and other things, governments are merely the products of culture. They are not culture by themselves. Culture determines what is acceptable or unacceptable, important or not important, right or wrong, workable or not workable."

Swami Vivekananda

According to Swami Vivekananda, "Culture is the Soul of a Nation. There is a lot of misconception about the word culture. Civilization should not be confused to mean culture. Culture is a characteristic way of life, inspired by fundamental values, according to which people live. It is the sum total of the values, expressed through art, literature, religion, social institutions and behavior, over acts of individuals and mass action inspired by collective urges. Culture is what we are, civilization is what we possess or what we make use of. Culture is the state of inner Man. His external expression is Civilization."

Chapter 1

Way of Life

No two cultures are same. The American and the Indian cultures are also two very different cultures. One of the major differences that can be seen, is in the family relations.

I went to India after 13 years in 2011. I have been living in Canada for about 40 years. During all this time, my hometown Ludhiana, has grown by 15 times to 3.5 million people. The city has about 1.5 million cars, almost one for every two persons.

During my trips to India in 2011 and in 2012, I was impressed with the interaction among people. My childhood friend, C.K. Maini was sick when I came to India in December of 2011. He was admitted to the Medanta Hospital in Delhi area, so I went to visit him. I was very much impressed with this modern hospital having about 1500 beds, clean, organized and equipped with most modern technology. I met about a dozen of C.K.'s friends and relatives in a large waiting area of the Hospital. Later on when C.K. came back home, I noticed many of his friends, neighbors and relatives visiting him regularly. **His wife Shashi and children, Sourabh and Surbhi, were also there all the time with him. Also**

number of people called on the phone, inquiring about his health.

From there, I went to Ludhiana and was looking to meet my school friend, Satinder. As he was not at his house, I noticed a man sitting across the street in his car, who told me that Satinder was out of town and that he will give my message to him upon his return. The same evening, I met my cousin for dinner that connected me to Satinder within 20 minutes by phone. This is what India is all about knowing, interacting and helping people.

This kind of interaction is not very common in America. People were offering all kinds of emotional support to C.K. at the hospital and at the house. The friendly neighbors and relatives become a big part of your life in India. People usually know what is going on with you and your family.

The life of Indians is centered around the families. Extended families often live together with two adult generations. Though, with the time, it is changing to a single family-living.

In American culture, one can see that the individuals think of self-reliance and independence. On the other hand, Indians are more dependent on others. While the children in USA are brought up to live an independent life, the children in India are brought up different way. In Indian culture, there is more respect for the older people and mostly it is they, who make the decisions. But in American culture, each individual makes his own decisions.

In India, there is very little privacy in smaller cities, though the big cities like Delhi and Mumbai are becoming more like western countries. There are good and bad things about both philosophies. I personally believe that the reasonable privacy is healthier. Complete isolation and being stranger, does not bring happiness and security in one's life.

Isolation, not sharing, does bring depression which causes many health related problems also. Many depressed people attempt suicide. Many famous people have attempted or suicided due to depression.

Recently, Michael Jackson's daughter, Paris Jackson, 15, attempted suicide.
Frank Sinatra, Drew Barrymore, Halle Berry, Elton John, Brittany Spear, Princess Diana, Clark Gable, Judy Garland, Eminem and many others attempted suicides.

Frank Sinatara

World Health Organization has identified depression as the major cause of suicides. Suicidal rate is very low in India. I think interaction and low expectations are the keys to avoid depression.

Children are very integral part of the Indian parent's lives. Their activities are centered on them. They are willing to sacrifice their most valuables for the education and well being of their children. This is much different in America.

Recently, I met a person at a wedding who has two married sons. A while ago, he bought a house for his eldest son. He told me, that he was looking to buy another

Indian child getting attention from grand parents

house for his second son who lived in another city. This is how the Indian parents think and feel responsible to establish their children. In turn, these children will do the same for their children. This tradition has been going on for centuries. This brings closeness, respect and security to the families.

In a Blog, Meeka, **an American, wrote, "I tried to be more the type that wants to be proud of and happy with what I have. My fiance (Indian) is more type that puts under lot of pressure to do well at school/work/home etc., and feels like he has to do better in life is what seems to motivate him. It seems that Indian parents just want their kids to be happy (settled, married, having kids, stable, close**

A Happy Family

to them). Western parents to 'find yourself' what you want to do/be and whatever that is."

While the Indians are very much family oriented, the Americans are individually oriented. In another sense, it can be said that the American culture is more goal oriented and the Indian culture is more people or family oriented. Indians may even forsake their own wishes and happiness for the sake of the families. But in American culture, this trend cannot be seen.

Unlike in America, where most of the relatives are called first or second cousin, uncle/aunt etc., in India, there are much defined names for each relation.

For example

Your father's elder brother will be called—	*Taya ji*
His wife will be called—	*Tai ji*
Your father's younger brother will be called	*Chacha ji*
His wife will be called—	*Chachi ji*
Your mother's brother will be called—	*Mama ji*
His wife will be called—	*Mami ji*
Your mother's sister will be called—	*Massi ji*
Her husband will be called—	*Massa ji*
Your brother's wife is called—	*Bhabhi ji*
Your wife's brother is called—	*Salla*
Your wife's sister is called—	*Salli*
Your mother-in-law will be called—	*Sass ji*
Your father-in-law will be called—	*Sassur ji*

and so on.

In the western world, many children leave their home at early age of 18-21 to pursue their life independently. The parents also encourage them, so that they have enjoyment of their own lives after raising the children.

Christina V. wrote in a blog, "in my life and so in most of my friend's lives, they can't rely on their families because family is dysfunctional."

Kate wrote—''as American, coming from an American point of view, I think that we do not have family as part of our happiness, is one of the saddest thing about our culture in comparison to Indian. **For now, I presently believe that India truly has something on America when it comes to family culture."**

To Indian parents, education of their children is the top priority, regardless whatever they have to do to support them, even selling their most valuable assets. This sacrifice is very rare in America. Indian teachers are also very dedicated to teach discipline to the students.

Parents do not complain as they know it is for the benefit to their children. It is a collective effort of parents and teachers to build the nation.

Women are more in number than men in schools and also at the higher education level in all the fields except in engineering, where they are catching up. Women are employed at the work places at equal level in all the fields including medical, engineering, finance, law, teaching, clerks and others.

In America, people emphasize more on sports. From the very beginning children are taught baseball, football, basketball, ice hockey etc. I have seen some parents getting up early Sunday mornings to take children to hockey practices in some arena; other parents take their children to baseball games. Weekends are mostly spent on sports or entertainments. Most of the parks in America are full of these young players practicing on their games. The parents always accompany and encourage them in their sports.

These outfits of the children are very expensive. For baseball outfit, it can cost anywhere $200-$1000, depending upon the size and quality of the outfit and the equipment. For ice-hockey, it is even more expensive. Good quality skating shoes alone can cost $500 or even more. Then to build these ice arenas are even more expensive for the government. I have seen some municipalities spending 50-60 million dollars on ice arenas. Football outfits are less expensive than ice-hockey outfits.

Children look at the success of professional players in America, making millions of dollars. Every time there is new recruitment in sports; the Leagues make it a very glamorous show. Big players, sign contracts for millions of dollars a year, which makes a big news. All the news papers, TV Stations and Sports Radio Shows, talk about it for a long time. There are some TV and Radio Stations who broadcast sports 24 hours a day. They talk about the performance of the players, the games and so on. There are lots of strategies in football and it is very interesting to listen and watch these talks.

Taking children to the games by the parents is very common in America. Baseball is the most famous game where eating hot dog is almost a must. Pop corn is also very popular with children and adults. Drinking lot of beer is a routine at the games. Of course, making noises and screaming is a lot of fun for all. I guess, that is the excitement and the way of life in America. Parents spend hundreds of dollars for each game for their children. In a blog somebody wrote ''Parents will spend more money on sports than on educating their children is a sad news.''

These games do teach discipline and team work to the children. Many CEO's have successfully used the strategy of games in managing their companies, very successfully.

Sports are the talks of every work place in America. I have heard a lot of discussions at the fast food restaurants, in offices. For many years, I have seen even little children and parents glued to the TV in the evenings to watch sports. It's amazing. Sports are also the talks at the dining tables.

These young children look forward to become professional players, broadcasters, and sports writers as these persons become very famous and make a lot of money. They are always on news, television, newspapers or on radio. The children set their goals and some of them succeed. The education becomes less of the priority.

The fact is that only 1-2% children succeed in making any dent in professional sports, because of which the children do not focus on their education. Even parents do not push their children towards education at the early age. It is too late for the children to focus on education by the time they are in higher grades in the schools. Many of them drop out of schools. There is very high dropout rate in high schools of America.

Recently on a radio talk show, a mother in USA commented "we are giving too much importance to sports and other activities while the Asians give priorities to math and science." She further said that this was the reason that Asians are making more progress than the Americans.

Children are also attracted to become musicians and singers. At early age, parents take them to glamorous shows and concerts. Children notice the lavish life styles of these stars with expensive wardrobes, expensive cars and houses. They visualize themselves to be one of them.

In America, most children have their own rooms where they spend lot of time alone. They have their own musical systems, TVs and computers. I have noticed some of them listening to the music all the time. Parents do not dare to go to the rooms of the grown up children for their privacy sake. Because of this, parents do not know what really is happening in their child's life.

Many children do fall in traps of these fake glamorous life styles of singers and actors, which take them away from the education. Education seems to be tougher than becoming a singer or a famous player for the children.

Looking at the Universities, large numbers of students come from other countries, or are born to the first generation immigrants.

In America, most students have to support themselves for their higher education, so they do part time or full time jobs. In many cases, this leads to diversion from the education to earning money. Once they get involved in a job, money flows easily. Some of them are less likely to pursue their goals of education and drop out of schools. Some of them get involved with alcohol and drugs. The bars are full of youngsters; some of them are school dropouts.

Recreation

Most American life and recreation is based on sports like football, baseball, basket ball etc. Most famous sports are the football, played nationally as well as at the University level. One in six Americans bets on sports. Men bet nearly twice as much as women on professional sports.

In general, Americans have less general knowledge about the world and their surroundings. Recently in a survey about the earth moving around sun, less than 10% American gave the right answer.

''Baseball, apple pie hot dog'' is a favorite phrase in America.

Happiness

''The US population as a whole is not getting happier'' Stevenson said ''for every unhappy person who becomes happier, there is someone on the other side conundrum down, money is probably not the driving force behind presumed happiness. American population as a whole is no longer happier that it was a decade ago.'' Stevenson and Wolfer used data collected from 1972-2006 from U of Chicago's General Social Welfare (*source*—U of Chicago, Journal of Legal Studies).

Author of the, Geography of Bliss, Eric Weiner wrote—**''many of us think that we have responsibility to be happy, but that is insane. Its why, we Americans suffer from what's called 'the unhappiness of not being happy.'** Nonetheless, mountains have been trapped, wisdom impaired and source of our current distress identified greed insatiable greed.''

Bhutan's Prime Minister declared greed to be the cause of current global economic meltdown and by extension our global unhappiness. **''We need to think Gross National Happiness,'' insists Jigme Thinley, Prime Minister of Bhutan.**

Jigme Thinley

Eric Weiner agrees with Bhutan's PM, but further he says **"source of unhappiness is expectations.** Greed fulfilled makes us happier for a while, but when our expectations are no longer met, we are miserable."

Michael J. Fox "your happiness grows in direct proportion to your acceptance and in inverse proportion to your expectations."

A Harvard Economist, Jeffery Sachs in his book, 'American Pursuit of Happiness' said "American GNP of $50,000/person and net worth of $500,000 per household are among the highest in the world, yet growing number of Americans are unhappy and increasingly pessimistic." Further he said, "one reason is obvious that income and wealth measures average what inequalities of income and wealth have reached all time high in America. **Top 1% of wealthy households have 90% of the wealth. Corporations own politicians, sports stadiums, medical systems, professional schools and universities and much of our military."**

It means the rest of the 99% of the population shares the 10% of the wealth in America bringing their net worth much lower? (According to the Economic Determination of Happiness, US General Social Survey).

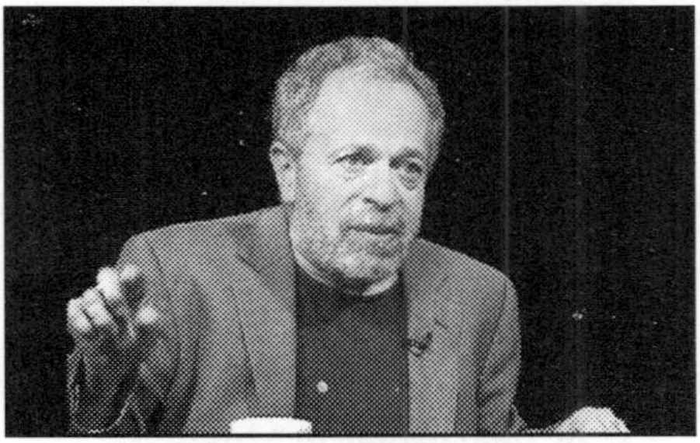

Robert Reich

Ex-Labor Secretary, Robert Reich, currently professor at University of California, Berkeley said, **"inequality is rising in America, 400 richest have more wealth than the bottom 150 million put together."** Which means one wealthy man in America has more wealth than the bottom 60,000 people put together? Mr. Reich was the Labor Secretary under President Clinton in 1990's.

Biggest factor of happiness is health.

- **Healthy people are 20% happier.**
- **Married people 10% happier than who never been married.**
- **People with higher income are 3.5% happier than average income earners.**
- **Inflation reduces happiness.**

In a blog, somebody asked a question "why in India, people do not decorate homes like in America."

Another person answered, "most have difficulty just making sure their life is in order and basic needs are met.

It is only after other factors have been taken care like -family life is stable, children are well educated and there is enough money etc., then they possibly think about superficial things such as decorating."

Sharell said "in west, we are not happier if our house is not looking as good as our friend's or neighbor's." (In daily life in India)

According to the study by Humanities Department of IIT of 2600 people in Mumbai:

Indian defines Happiness as—"Peace and Harmony" American—"Joy and Enthusiasm"

In India—Relationship is a major consi-deration, well being is defined by the growth of other people's lives. This is due to collective rather than individ-ualistic nature of the Indian society.

In America—Relationship is defined by friends and work. Well being is defined by individualism, family does not get mentioned in the west.

Unlike the Indians, the Americans plan things ahead.

Americans believe in dominating and controlling the world around them.

On the contrary Indians believe in the harmony.

Another difference that can be seen between Indian culture and American culture is that the:

Indians love stability

Americans love mobility.

Americans have great regard for time and its value which Indians are lacking.

Coming to competition, Indians are more competitive than the Americans.

Coming to work nature, the Indians work for meeting the family needs.

On the contrary, Americans will only strive to rise on his own capacity or getting rich.

Religion

India is the birthplace of Hinduism, Buddhism, Jainism and Sikhism, collectively known as Indian religions

(Dharma), are a major form of world religions. Today, According to a 2002 Census of India, the religion of 80% of the people is Hinduism. Islam in India is the second largest religion with over 135 million Muslims. The country celebrates Eid as a public holiday.

Christianity is India's third largest religion with over 23 million Christians. India is the home to many Christian festivals. The country celebrates Christmas and Good Friday as public holidays.

Food

Each part of the country has its own cuisine. Food is bought and consumed the same day in India. Even families with refrigerators, typically use them to keep water, soft drinks, or milk cool. This is different in USA where most of the food is either frozen or refrigerated for few days.

Social visiting is mainly with relatives and friends who are entertained at homes in India. Youngsters meet at the restaurants or tea stalls to socialize. In America, usually, people entertain guests at the restaurants.

Clothing

The basic clothing for most women is the sari. Styles of tying the sari vary among regions and communities. Saris are generally colorful and can be made of cotton or the finest embroidered silks.

Men in the offices, at management level, wear like in any other western country, a 2 piece suit, office staff is

neatly dressed. The offices are very modern with up to date technology of computers, lap tops etc. Number of cell phones in India are double than entire population of the United States.

Men in general wear shirt/pant or Kurta/Pajama. Tight-fitting style is often worn with a long closed-collar coat (the sherwani) made famous in the West when India's first Prime Minister, Jawaharlal Nehru, wore it. It is also called the Nehru Jacket. It is the most formal dress for men. Turbans are worn by a broad range of men, especially Sikhs and Hindus. Muslims can often be identified by their embroidered caps.

Sports and Entertainment

India's National Cricket team competes at the highest international level. Soccer is popular in Eastern India. In Central India men play a Indian team sport, Kabaddi, that requires quickness and strength. The oldest sport, one that goes back to the time of the Hindu epics, is Freestyle Wrestling. Wrestling clubs, presided over by a guru, feature a regiment of Hindu religious ritual and practice.

Sachin Tendulkar is a former Indian cricketer widely acknowledged as the greatest batsman of the modern generation, popularly holds the title 'God of Cricket' among his fans. He is also acknowledged as the greatest cricketer of all time. He took up cricket at the age of eleven, made his Test debut at the age of sixteen, and went on to represent India for close to twenty four years. He is the only player to have scored one hundred international centuries, the first batsman to score a Double Century in a One Day International, and the only player to complete more than 30,000 runs in international cricket. In October 2013, he became the 16th player and first Indian to aggregate 50,000 runs in all recognized cricket. Recently **he was awarded BHARAT RATNA the highest Indian Civilian Award.**

Sachin Tendulkar

There are a number of traditional games played mainly by men. These include Chess, which originated in India, and Pachisi, which literally means 'twenty-five,' after the number of spaces moved in one throw of the dice in

Vishwanathan Anand : Chess

the original Indian game. Card games also are common as is gambling.

Indian Cinema

Most Indians like to go to the cinemas for entertainment or watch television. Younger generation is fond of fast foods in India.

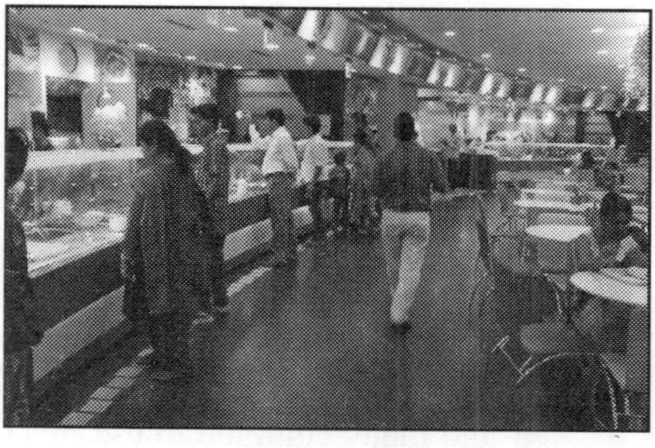

Indian Fastfood Restaurant

During school holidays families may visit relatives or go briefly to hill resorts where it is cooler in the summer. In rural areas, slack times in the agricultural cycle allow families to go on pilgrimage or attend weddings, which include much feasting.

Marriages

Arranged marriages are less and less popular in India now a days. Some of the marriages are still planned by their parents and other respected family-members. I have seen in our families in India, most of the youngsters selected their own life partners.

Scene of a Wedding

Michelle wrote in a blog, on the subject of arranged marriages and others, ‘‘having an arranged marriage is not a bad idea if it is done with right motivation. Our children are very spoiled. They have a sense of entitlements. Some parents will put themselves in debt to indulge their whims not for the education but for toys.’’

Namaste, Namaskar is a common spoken greeting or salutation, though being considered old-fashioned by some. Namaskar is considered a slightly more formal version than Namaste but both express deep respect. It is commonly used in India by Hindus, Jains and Buddhists, and many continue to use this outside the Indian subcontinent. In Indian culture, the word is spoken at the beginning of written or verbal communication. However, by the folded hands, gesture is made usually wordlessly upon departure.

Festivals

India, being a multi-cultural and multi-religious society, celebrates holidays and festivals of various religions. The four National holidays in India, the Independence Day, the Republic Day, the Gandhi Jayanti, and May Day are celebrated across India.

In addition, many Indian states and regions have local festivals. **Popular religious festivals include the Hindu festivals of Diwali, Ganesh Chaturthi, Durga puja, Holi, Raksha-bandhan, and Dussehra.**

Certain festivals in India are celebrated by multiple religions. Notable examples include Diwali, which is celebrated by Hindus, Sikhs and Jains, and Buddh Purnima, cele-brated by Buddhists. Sikh Festivals, such as Guru Nanak Jayanti, Baisakhi are celebrated with full fanfare by Sikhs and Hindu, adding colors to the culture of India. Muslims celebrate Eid in a big way all over India.

Vedas

According to Indian traditions, ''God gave the wisdom in the form of Vedas to four Rishis.''

1. Agni Rishi got the knowledge of **Rig Veda**
2. Vaayu Rishi of **Yajur Veda**
3. Aaditya Rishi of **Saama Veda** and
4. Angira Rishi of **Atharva Veda**

These Vedas are called 'Shruti'. The source of Vedic knowledge is God and not human, according to Dr. Balvir Acharya, internationally renowned Vedic scholar and former professor and Head of the Department at MD University, Rohtak, India.

The fundamental message of the Vedas is universal. Vedas teach to promote physical, spiritual and social development of the entire mankind without any discrimination of cast, color, creed, religion, race or sex. The Vedas promote universal brotherhood.

1. **Rig Veda:** Rig Veda is called the 'Veda of Knowledge or Jnyaan Kaand.' This Veda has ten Mandals, 1028 Sukta and total of 10,552 Mantras. It contains physical, spiritual, philosophical and social knowledge.

2. **Yajur Veda:** Yajur Veda primarily contains the description of various rituals and yajnas. It is therefore called the 'Veda of Action or Karma Kaand.' Yajur Veda has 40 chapters and 1,975 Mantras.

3. **Saama Veda:** Sama Veda primarily has the knowledge of music and spiritual practices such as Bhakti. Hence it is also called 'Upaasanaa Kaand.' This Veda contains 1,875 Mantras.

4. **Atharva Veda:** Atharva Veda has the knowledge of Universe, our solar system, the oceans, the continents, politics, aayurveda, naturopathy, treatment with water, celibacy and other subjects dealing with physical science. It is, therefore, called the 'Veda of Sciences or Vijyaana Kaand.' This Veda has 20 Kaanda, 731 Sukta and a total of 5,977 Mantras.

Sanskars

According to Dr. Balvir Acharya, Sanskars are the sum of three things—"the actions of the previous birth, genetics of parents and family we are born in, and in the environment we live in ever since birth." It is believed that by proper guidance and appropriate conduct, it is possible to change the Sanskars or the character of an individual. This is what the Sanskar system is all about.

Dr. Acharya has described the following 16 Sanskars:

1. **Garbhaadhan Sanskar:** this is performed when the married couple decides to have a child. The expected mother is absorbed in such thoughts, which she would desire her offspring to imbibe and absorb.

2. **Punsavan Sanskar:** this is performed after 2-3 months of conception for the good development of the fetus.

3. **Seemantonnavan Sanskar:** this is for the mental development of the child.

4. **Jaat-karma Sanskar:** this is performed at birth. Baby is cleaned, bathed and OM is written on the tongue with Ghee and Honey.

5. **Naamkaran Sanskar:** this is performed some time after birth when a name is given to the baby. Significance of the name is to create a positive perception.

6. **Nishkraman Sanskar:** this Sanskar is given to take the blessings of God.

7. **Anna-Praashan Sanskar:** this is performed when teething has begun and the child is being weaned from mother's milk and solid food is going to be introduced.

8. **Chudaa-Karma (Mundan) Sanskar:** this is performed in 1st to 3rd year of life. Hair is cut first time of the baby. The significance of this is to draw attention of parents towards the mental and spiritual development of the child.

9. **Karma-Veda Sanskar:** this is not really performed as a Sanskar in modern times.

10. **Upanayan Sanskar:** this marks the start of pursuit of knowledge. This Sanskar is performed between 8-12 years of age.

11. **Vedarambh Sanskar:** this Sanskar stresses the importance of both material and spiritual knowledge. Special emphasis is given to the avoidance of anger.

12. **Samaavartan Sanskar:** this is a Graduation Ceremony performed at the age of 14.

13. **Vivah Sanskar:** this is the marriage ceremony. In the ceremony seven steps are taken by the couple around fire (Havan Kund). During ceremony, rice which have not been husked, are offered. This symbolizes the growth of the harvested rice when it is replanted, which relate to the bride because she is taken from her home and

flourish in her new home with her husband.

14. **Vanprastha Sanskar:** this is the first stage of detachment from material possessions. This is designed to give back to the community and concentrate in social work.

15. **Sanyas:** in this and last stage of life, one is detached from all actions, where fruit is desired. These are teachings of Vedas, Upanishads and Gita. In modern world context, it should not really require one to leave home. Here one is to do more of introspection, meditation and social service.

16. **Antyeshti:** this is performed after death where physical body is offered back to nature with God's blessings. The soul leaves the body at the time of death and takes the subtle and causal bodies with it. After death, Atma enters the emptiness of cosmos, and as preordained according to its karma, either takes a new birth or achieves salvation or MOKSHA.

Hindus Believe

Soul cannot be wounded by weapons, neither can it be burnt by fire, water cannot wet it. Salvation is the ultimate goal of existence. In Hindu philosophy, there are three external elements: God, Soul and Nature. God is Omnicient, Omni present and less born and the creature of the Universe, according to Dr. Balvir Acharya.

Hindutva believes that the present life is the fruit of Karma accrued in the previous births. The next birth is the follow up of the present birth. You reap the fruit of your labor, whether it is sweet or sour.

The Hindu way of life believes that the soul is imprisoned in the body. It is engulfed in ignorance. Ignorance is the cause of sorrow. Therefore, its sole aim is deliverance from this imprisonment through the attainment of knowledge and ultimately get fused with the universal soul. Hindu believes that God exists in every living being.

Life in India is based on the dual principle of Service and Sacrifice. These are kinds of Yajnas performed throughout life. Earnings, savings and enjoying are governed by certain social rules.

Our focus is not on our rights, but on our duties. Rights and powers are the results of western ways of thinking which has resulted in cut-throat competition, friction, jealousy and hatred. This has resulted in the breakup of the joint family system in India.

There is no question of power in Hindutva. A certain form of sacredness is attached to the duty and service. It is termed as dharma. We have concepts such as putra (son's) dharma, pita (father's) dharma, patni (wife's) dharma, sevaka (follower's) dharma, swamy (teacher's) dharma, vidyarthi (student's) dharma etc. Our society became well established as a result of these dharmas.

Peaceful co-existence is the cornerstone of Hindu life. We have innumerable religious, castes, languages, customs and beliefs still they coexist. To a westerner, this phenomenon is unbelievable. The basis of such a life is found in the **Rigveda which says "walk together, speak together, think and reason together. Your ancestors have lived like this and followed certain practices, according to their abilities and needs."**

Dr. D. P. Maini

In the book 'The Indian Values', Dr. D.P.Maini, a well known professor at the Punjab University, described:

Indians basically believe in diligent life. Being believers in the philosophy of action, they know that they will definitely reap the fruit of their actions, may be immediately or later on. He has respect for mother, father, preceptor and elderly people. This is only way to pay the debt that is due to mother, father and God.

For the inoculation of good qualities, children are given good and meaningful names. Indians believe in the unity of name, beauty and shape. Therefore, study of doctrines, noble actions and noble company has got special meaning for them.

Hospitality is a special feature of Indian life. A guest is looked after with great care and his blessings are always sought. To take care of the old and sick is our humanitarian duty. The service which generates ego has no place in Indian life. Donations should be given with honesty and selflessness.

The gift of knowledge is considered the highest form of gift. It is necessary that a house and the occupants are neat and clean, simple and appealing. Character has got more value than the nature of clothes.

Patience, forgiveness, austerity, non-stealing, purity, control of senses, intellect, knowledge, truth and avoidance of anger makes a person sublime. Knowing oneself entails discovering one's own nature. Temperament, natural tendencies, inclinations and inner faculties are part and parcel of one's personality.

Karma

On the subject of Karma, Dr. Maini who has written 18 books, described that the fruit of action is of three kinds:

1. **Present Actions—**while performing actions we receive the fruit. As we pluck a mango from a tree, in the same way, we receive the fruit of our actions.

2. **Collected Actions—**after working hard one collects a small amount, deposits it in the bank and it accumulates interest and then becomes a large amount in ten years time. By obtaining education in fourteen or fifteen years, one gathers knowledge and becomes specialist in a subject, so is the situation with the fruit after accumulated action.

3. **Destiny—**is called the fruit of those actions which are collected actions beyond present and past, and go along with us not only in this life but in the next life as well.

Linda Johnsen wrote in her book, Hinduism, "Hindus remain among the most and hospitable people on the earth, the guest is God," she said. "In India, women's role perceived to be very different than in North America."

"During first 60 years, nearly 25% of the time, India was ruled by a woman Prime Minister. Since freedom for more than 230 years, America has never been ruled by a female President. In India, women's name is taken first like, Sita-Ram, Radhe-Krishan." Ms. Johnsen wrote.

Indian culture is superior to the American culture.

●

Chapter 2

Education

The education has been defined as: It is a form of learning in which the knowledge, skill and habits of a group of people are transferred from one generation to the next through teaching, trading or research.

In a blog, Brian Nicole expressed his opinion on the benefits of the education is, that:

- The education will start you thinking positive
- The education will make you a better decision maker.
- The salary range will increase with more education.
- The chance of being hired will increase.
- I will be able to choose where I want to work, not just take a job, because I have to survive.

The basic education starts at home and at the elementary level of a school where the children learn the fundamentals. During my recent trips to India, **I visited many schools in different cities, including Delhi, and learned that the children there knew the multiplication tables, shapes, additions/subtractions at much earlier level than in USA.**

I heard an elementary school teacher, talking to his friends in a restaurant in America, saying that many of the students in his class already knew subjects he was teaching. He further said that their parents already taught many of the subjects to these Asian students at an early age and that he did not had to work hard to teach them the same subjects. He loved his job.

Many teachers in India told me that the children know these multiplication tables when they are in Grade 2-3, as the parents take interest and teach them at an early age. These tables are taught in Grades 5-6, in America. They also know alphabetical in English as well in the local regional language at Kindergarten.

I noticed a similar trend with Indian-American parents in America, that they kept the same traditions. This was obvious from the Scripps National Spelling Bee Competition in USA for a decade, where about 50% championship titles are won by the Indian children.

In 2009, Kavya Shivshankar won Scripps National Spelling Bee competition among some 250 competitors from all over the world. There were 7 Indian children out of 11 finalists. This competition reflects the intelligence of the children. Kavya was very happy and in an interview with the press stated ‘‘my homecoming was

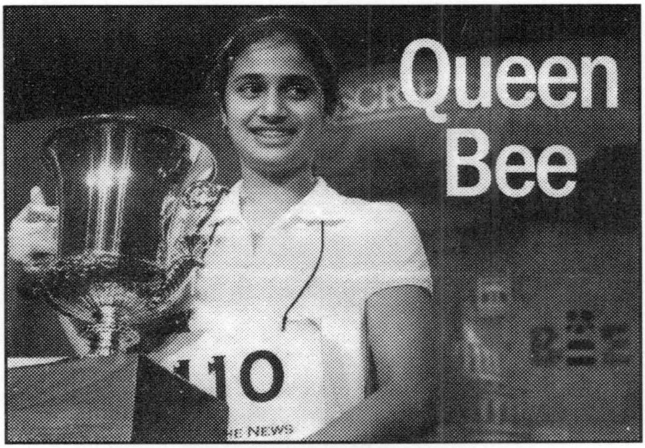

Kavya Shivshankar
won Scripps National Spelling Bee Competition in 2009

covered live from a Helicopter.'' **Many of the top news reporters of America stated that Indians are one of the most intelligent people in the world.**

The Indian parents and teachers are one of the most dedicated people in the world. They believe that education is the best asset for the children which will stay with them forever, anything else is not as reliable. The poor are even more particular about it as they want their children to have a better life than their own. This is the dedication ''Better than their own life.'' The children notice their parents working hard all their lives to make the ends meet. They also want a high paying job by getting better education.

The teaching starts at homes in India at an early age of 3 or 4, when parents start teaching alphabetical and additions/subtractions to the children. It becomes more or less fun for children. By the time the kids are six or seven, they know most of the tables etc., besides recognizing shapes, colours, tell time which they have learned even earlier.

In 2010 Another American-Indian, Aadith Moorthy 13, won the National Geography Bee in Washington, D.C.

Dr Amit Mitra

Dr Amit Mitra, Secretary - General, Federation of Indian Chambers of Commerce and Industry, He did his Masters in Economics from Delhi School of Economics in 1970 and then obtained a Doctorate in Economics from Duke University, USA in 1978. He has taught at major universities in the United States. **"Now, Americans perceive Indians to be smart.** The infotech revolution changed it all," he said.

Har Gobind Khorana

Noble Prize Winner Har Gobind Khorana born in Raipur Village, Punjab in India was a biochemist who shared the 1968 Nobel Prize for Physiology or Medicine with Marshall W. Nirenberg and Robert W. Holley. Khorana and Nirenberg were also awarded the Louisa Gross Hurwitz Prize from Columbia University in the same year.

He became a naturalized citizen of the United States in 1966, and subsequently received the National Medal of Science. He served as MIT's Alfred P. Sloan Professor of Biology and Chemistry, Emeritus and was a member of the Board of Scientific Governors at The Scripps Research Institute.

In an article published in The Times of India in 2012 with headlines,'US Colleges Learn Business Mantras from Indian Gurus'. It named:

Soumitra Dutta
Dean, Ivy League Cornell University.

Nitin Nohria
Dean, Harvard Business School.

Dipak Jain
Dean, Kellogg School of Management, and so many others.

Vijay Govindarajan

Top management thinker and professor of International Business at the Tuck School of Business, Darmouth College, **Vijay Govindarajan,** agreed that the Indian management professors have an edge in being educated in English as well versed in western pedagogues. **"We are the Masters of Data and Facts."**

Most of these professors had their basic education in India, where parents and teachers grind the students with basics of education at an early age, including multiplication tables, alphabetical.

A program "Common core state standard initiative" published by **Michigan Department of Education** shows the standard of math from K-6 grades:

(*a*) **Grade 1 and 2**

In American teachings—recognizing and comparing two dimensional figures, solving the word problem like you have two dimes and three pennies, how many cents do you have?

In Indian teachings—most of the children know these in Kindergarten plus numbers spellings 1-100 (oral).

(*b*) **Grade 3**

In American teachings—to tell time in interval of time, solve word problem involving additions and subtractions of time interval.

In Indian teachings—these are taught in grade 1 & 2. Plus number spellings 0-200 written and 0-300 oral, tables 1 to 20, multiplications, divisions (in decimal) and additions, subtractions (in decimal).

(*c*) **Grade 4, 5, 6**

In American teachings—multiplications, divisions, additions, subtractions and others.

These are taught by grade 2-3 in India.

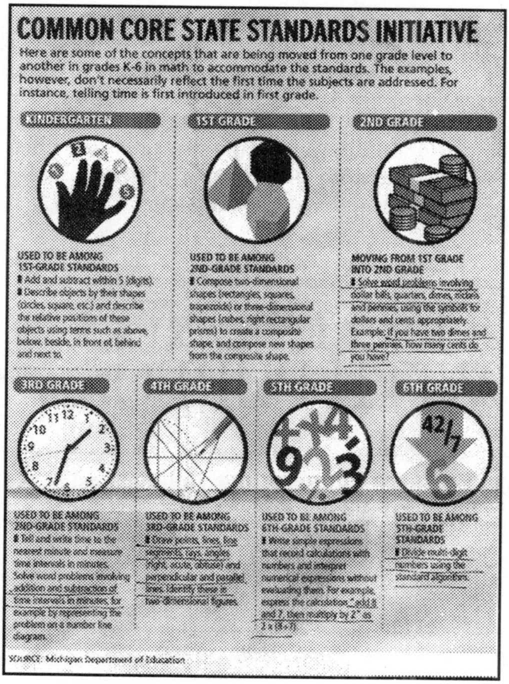

Curriculum comparison of schools in USA - India
Michigan(USA) Dept of Education (2012)

Kindergarten	**Add and Subtract 5 digits Describe objects by shapes & describe their relative positions**
Grade - I	**Compose 2 & 3 dimensional shapes and combine them to form composite shapes**
Grade - II	**Solve word problems involving Dollar bills, quarters, dimes, nickels and pennies using symbol for dollar and cents appropriately.**
Grade - III	**Tell and write time to the nearest minute and measure time intervals in minutes. Solve word problems involving addition and subtraction of time intervals in minutes.**
Grade - IV	**Draw Points, line segments, rays, angles and perpendicular and parallel lines. Identify these in two-dimensional figures. (Taught in second grade in India)**
Grade - V	**Write simple expressions that record calculations with numbers and interpret numerical expressions without evaluation. (Taught in second grade in India)**
Grade - VI	**Divide multi digit numbers using the standard algorithm. (Taught in third grade in India)**

Source - Michigan Department of Education.

India - Central Board of Secondary Education (2013)

Kindergarten	**Alphabet A-Z, in Capital and Running hand Number spellings upto 100 Oral Vowels General Knowledge - Nature**
Grade - I	**Sentence formation, Number spellings upto 100 written, Number spellings upto 200 Oral Addition-Subtraction 1-99 Tables 1-6, Time and currency counting Computer Theory and Practical**
Grade - II	**Stories, Poems, Big Sentence formation Number spellings upto 200 written Number spellings upto 300 Oral Addition-Subtraction in Decimals Multiplication-Division in Decimals Tables 1-20, Computer Theory and Practical**
Grade - III	**Stories, Big Lessons, Grammar, Full Sentence formation Fractional Number, Shape, Addition, Subtracting upto 6 digits**
Grade - IV	**Big Paragraph, Comprehension, Essay, Letter-Application writing, Full Grammar, Opposites, Full Addition-Subtraction Multiplication-Division Geometry and handling big data**
Grade - V	**Big Essay, Writting about picture, Application (Formal/Informal) Full Grammar, Big Sums, Geometry and handling big data Number system (Binary,Decimal,Octal,Hexadecimal).**
Grade - VI	**Big Story, Full Grammar, Message/Notice, Story/diary, Report writing, Algebra, Big Number system Trigonomentry, Practical Geometry, Measurement, Data Base Management**

According to Dr. Ravish Mishra (author of 13 books)
Principal D.A.V. Public School, Gandhidham - Gujarat

Students are known to be more rowdy in the class rooms of American schools. Many teachers do not feel safe. One school Board in Michigan, with about 10,000 students, had over 1000 assaults in one year including many physical assaults.

Large amount of money, up to $12,000 per student per year, is being spent by various governments on the education in America. Big chunk of this amount goes to

wages, pensions and the benefits of the teachers. This expenditure has been increasing disproportion to the total budget. In Michigan, the percentage of payroll dollars spent on retirement benefits skyrocketed from 13% to 27% in just 10 years, from 2003-2013. In a payroll of one billion dollars, these expenses can increase from $130 million to $270 million. This money has to come from somewhere, either in an increase in the property taxes or reducing library facilities, sports activities, compromising safety or poor building maintenance and may be in reduction of some other student facilities.

The greed has taken over in the schools of America. Many teachers made the same amount of money in pensions after the retirement, which they were making, just few years earlier, while working full time.

Recently, I was listening to a radio talk show, where a man was blaming the teachers, being selfish for their high wages and pensions that might have caused the death of a 14 year old student, crossing the road across from the school. He was pointing out the absence of a

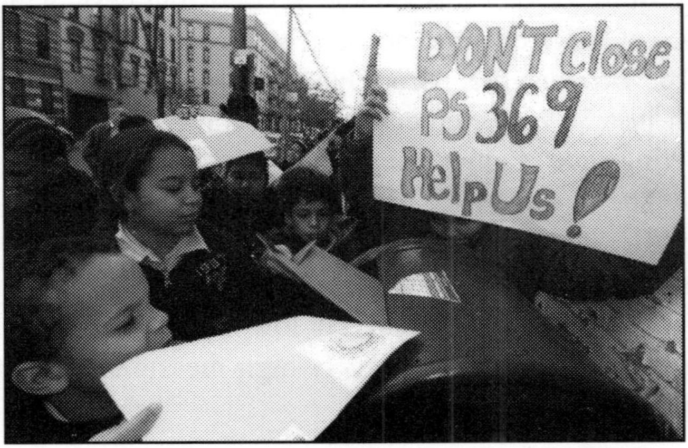

patrol guard for the students to cross the road. He said the school boards had cut the budget which compromised the safety and other issues of the students.

The south Bronx and Central Brooklyn are the toughest spots to be a kid in the city, according to a new report from the Citizens' Committee for Children.

The non-profit ranked neighborhoods based on indicators of childhood success and happiness such as reading scores, child abuse rates, and child poverty rates.

The results shine a light on the neediest parts of the city, where resources are scarce, said Committee director Jennifer March-Joly.

"More attention must be paid to the needs of children and families, where barriers to child well-being are the greatest," March-Joly said.

Hunts Point was ranked the toughest place for the city's kids, with a 49 % child poverty rate and just 28% of elementary and middle school students meeting state reading standards in 2011.

Mott Haven was ranked second toughest, with 99 cases of reported child abuse or neglect per 1,000 kids in 2010. Brownsville, Brooklyn was ranked third worst, with just 28% of elementary and middle school students meeting state reading standards.

The Upper East Side, Tottenville, Staten Island and Bayside, Queens were top-ranked neighborhoods for raising kids, according to the report.

Those areas had relatively low rates of child poverty and child abuse, and relatively high measures of student achievement.

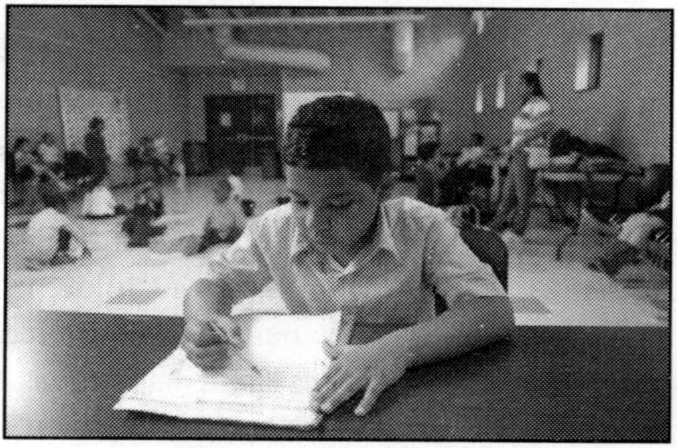

Eight-year-old Kenneth Morales does homework at Mitchel Community Center in Mott Haven in the Bronx. Mott Haven was ranked second toughest in the study, with 99 cases of reported child abuse or neglect per 1,000 kids in 2010.

On CNN's Anderson Cooper's show, in October of 2013, one Senator said that the education system has failed in America.

Rick Snyder

Governor of Michigan, Rick Snyder said ''Education in the State is Broken. We have built up a system that does not work anymore in terms of helping people to be successful," as per Detroit Free Press on April 23, 2013.

President Obama, in his State of the Union Address of 2013, said ''today, skyrocketing cost keeps too many

young people out of a higher education or saddle them with unsustainable debt. Colleges must do the part to keep costs down and it's our job to make sure that they do."

Mother of Steve Jobs, taught him how to read before he went to school. Later, Mr. Jobs created the most valuable company of the world, Apple Inc.

Steve Jobs

Ratings of the world's universities are inconsistent. They have ranked the Indian Universities below 200. IIT's of India are well known universities in the world. Many companies including Microsoft, NASA, InfoTech and others have recruited the graduates from these Institutes in large number.

Indian Institute of Technology : Roorkee

One of the major benefits of education is getting well paid and secured job. That is only possible, if the employer feels that you are qualified of doing the required work. Even the Governors and Senators have said that American education system does not work anymore. This is a further proof that many of the Indian universities are much better than the universities of USA, as large number of these graduates are employed in highly paid jobs in America.

Even Brian Nicole, quoted above (top of this article) on the benefits of the education, says, ''having better chance of being hired and to have better salary range.'' This is exactly what graduates from IIT India and from other Indian universities are getting in America. I believe, the world rating system of the universities, need to be re-evaluated.

Education has a very significant role to play in the lives of the people which can change the culture of a country.

Indian school education is better than the American education which makes the Indian culture superior to the American culture.

●

Chapter 3

Yoga and Meditation

Nixon had phlebitis and was excruciating pain on a visit to India. A well known yoga expert, Bikram Choudhury, was summoned to help. He gave some poses to ease the pain and Nixon was so impressed that he invited him to come to the U.S.

Dr. D. Ornish, a personal physician of President Bill Clinton since 1993, advised him to do yoga, meditation and half hour walk daily to keep healthy. Doctor Ornish stated in an interview with CBS.

Dr. Oz

Dr. Oz and Dr. Roizen advised to do 10 minutes of meditation twice a day to reduce lower back pain, reduce stress and anxiety, according to an article in Toronto Star.

"To keep your body physically and mentally fit, yoga exercise is a must," according to Dr. Balvir Acharya, internationally renowned Vedic scholar and former professor and Head of the Department at MD University, Rohtak, India.

"Medical science has concluded that to keep healthy, one should do regular yoga. Health of the body depends to a great extent on the state of mind. Negative thoughts adversely affect the body. Until now, medical science is unable to find the solution to remove negative thoughts from the mind. Only yoga can do it. Positive thoughts bring happiness," Dr. Acharya said who wrote several books on Yoga and Meditation.

In USA, there are about 25,000 outlets teaching yoga. In 2001 there were about 4 million people, including many celebrities, doing yoga regularly which has increased to 20 million by 2011 in America.

Louise Hay, the famous writer of the book 'You can heal your life' whose more than 40 million copies sold worldwide, learned Transcendental yoga at Maharishi Int'l University in Fairfield, Iowa at the age of 75. **She does yoga at least three times a week. She advises to sit quietly for few minutes, every day,** and observe the breath as it goes in and out of your body.

Louise Hay

Bill Ford, Madonna, Goldie Hawn, Jennifer Aniston and many others are regularly doing yoga believing it is strengthening muscles and effect aging.

British Comedian, Russel Brand, 37, loves his daily yoga sessions because he finds it ''highly psychological and very beautiful.'' He had battled with drug and sex addiction, is very regular in doing yoga and the techniques ''overwhelming.''

Mary MacVean wrote in Los Angeles Times, under the heading, Meditation Goes Mainstream, ''I was in the midst of five days of silence, 2, 4 and 5 were not much different. I'm not the quiet type. With the direction to attend only to our breathing, if you lose track, teacher Howard Cohn said, just return to it, without judgment, one of many easier said than done instructions I heard during my five days of silence;

"I breathed in. Suddenly, I was sorting out details of a dinner I was giving when I go back to L.A. Oops. Back to the breathing. One breath may be two, and my mind was off again, wondering about my son's trip to Israel. But I kept at it. After all, we came the wayward children our minds can often be." Not talking turn out to be easy. Meditation, however, is hard work, "it's spiritual but not religious. The idea is to gain clarity, wisdom and freedom, to end up feeling compelled to behave with integrity and compression." Mary said.

The word Yoga stems from the Sanskrit root "Yuj", meaning integration or the union of the mind and body. According to the Hindu philosophy and Vedas, "this involves the control of facilities of mind."

Yoga practices as prescribed by Sage Patanjali, coupled with a life style that include proper intake of food and other natural substances such as water regularly, then the success is definitely within reach.

Lord Krishna

Hindu holy book, "Gita" described Yoga as being able to perform our duties effectively and without an eye on the corresponding rewards, and furthermore, being in a state that one remains unperturbed while experiencing the opposites of the state.

Prenatal Yoga

Kristin McGee, a celebrity trainer said ''just because you are a mom, you can still rock cute outfit, that hug your curves, don't hide in a baggy clothes, prenatal yoga has helped, she said. ''it's specifically structured with poses that fights the discomfort of pregnancy and high lights relations and breathing exercise to cut stress.''

Indian tradition divides Yoga into 8 disciplines, according to Dr. Acharya:

1. Yama—Yama is the social code of the followings:

(*a*) **Ahinsa** (non-violence): Not to hurt any living being, bodily or mentally by our thoughts, words, and deeds in Ahinsa.

(*b*) **Saty** (truthfulness): As it has been heard or that transpires within, or that has been heard only that should be cognized off and uttered, this is Saty. When a person behaves with full confidence, honesty both in words and in action, he can achieve success easier in any of his endeavors in life.

(*c*) **Astey** (non-stealing): One should not harbor the idea to obtain somebody's belongings by thoughts, word, or deeds and through conceit, injustice and without the master's approval.

(*d*) **Brahmacharya** (celibacy): When a person practices celibacy, mentally, in words and actions, one can obtain physical and intellectual might. Once the body is stronger, the person is free of diseases and can live longer.

(*e*) **Aparigrah** (not to hoard): One should not collect things beyond legitimate requirements. Once a person learns to practice aparigrah, he becomes curious to know the inner self, such as who I am, where I come from, where will I go, what are my duties etc. it is these questions which can lead to self-realization.

2. Niyam—or the rules for yourself:

(*a*) **Shauch** (cleanliness): Means to remain clean both inside and outside. Body must be cleaned every day. Cleanliness can result in increasing peace of mind and can be happy and focused.

(*b*) **Santosh** (contentment): The happiness which results from self-satisfaction is better than any other happiness in life. When a calamity arises, a person who remains contended is less unhappy compared to others.

(*c*) **Tap** (austerity): In performing duties, one should not be perturbed on account of the extremes of pleasure-pain, cold-hot etc. and sail through them unperturbed. By following this, person becomes more healthy, strong and energetic.

(*d*) **Swaadhyaaya** (self study and study of scriptures): Means study of lofty literature, including the study of Yoga and to attain Salvation.

(*e*) Ishwar pranidhaan (surrender to God): This can help a person get deeper in meditation.

3. Aasan (posture, stretching exercising): Postures form body exercises to obtain body health. The strength to tolerate hunger, weather and other calamities increases as well. The blood circulation in the body is better with better body metabolism and easier rival of toxin from the body.

4. Pranayama (exercise of breadth): This means magnifying the vital breath giving rise to mental stability, body cleansing and intellectual development. By practicing Pranayama, the ignorance and bad habits are lost, the person begin to know the real truth and becomes a better human being.

5. Pratyahaar (detachment of worldly objects): Pratyahaar is to bring the sense organs away from the worldly affairs in a restful state as that of the mind. One can experience lasting peace and happiness. The mind is focused further and one is more conscious towards his responsibility.

6. Dhaarana (concentration): Once the external limbs of Yoga have been acquired, then it becomes easier to anchor the mind at a safe point and this is called Dhaarana. In this stage a person can experience even deeper sense of peace and happiness.

7. Dhyaayan (meditation): In this stage, the mind is concentrating at naval, throat and heart. The mind is totally focused and negative thoughts are completely removed. The person is able to successfully complete most responsibilities in life.

8. Samaadhi (communion): The ultimate climax in the state of Dhyaayan is called Samaadhi. In this state, a person is free from all unhappiness and experiences the state of bliss.

The basic principle of yoga is to bring about

harmony of the mind, body, and spirit, resulting in holistic therapy. Yoga also focuses on detoxification of the body, and the poses help in improving overall strength and flexibility.

Currently in America, yoga is exercised by sitting like aasan pose which is correct way of doing it, If all the yoga exercises are done carefully, it can cure many mental and physical problems.

Baba Ramdev

Baba Ramdev is known as Yoga Guru. Baba Ramdev has popularized Yoga in India at mass level. He studied Indian scriptures, Sanskrit and Yoga. He has helped people curing many diseases such as Heart disease, Arthritis, Blood Pressure, and many more without the use of any medication.

He has taught yoga to many actors including Amitabh Bachchan and Shilpa Shetty. He has also

Shilpa Shetty

taught yoga in the British Parliament, at the MD Anderson Cancer Center affiliated to the University of Texas. Apart from making Yoga a household word in India, he has also taught Yoga in USA and Japan among other countries.

From the beginning Baba Ramdev had aimed to build a "Yoga Aashram." Baba Ramdev has deep knowledge of

Samkhya philosophy and the Bhagavad Gita. Yoga taught by Baba Ramdev consists of Yoga Sutra from their ancient holy granth. Baba Ramdev focuses on achieving Samadhi by practicing meditation (Pranayam). This can be achieved by following the eight disciplines that are Yama, Niyama, Asana, Pranayama, Pratyahara, Dhaarana, Dhayana and Samadhi. Baba Ramdev is the icon of yoga of Pranayama and renowned Yoga teacher and an Ayurveda Guru. Today Baba Ramdev is considered to be a phenomenon not only in India but also abroad.

Meditation and Stock Market

Money is one of the top three things that seriously stress people. "Realistically, the only thing the stress and worry achieve is to cause you discomfort, nothing truly positive comes out of it" as posted in an article in Meditation Techniques.

"This is where meditation, especially mindful meditation, comes on. The meditation gives you an amazing ability to become calm. When you get into calm state, you are able to release all of the negative junk, the negative baggage that you carry with you."

"Meditation also helps you to begin and be positive again. In actual fact you get double from it. The negatives just disappear, zero lingering effect. So you become positive at faster rate than normal," the article said.

In a blog in 2010, "Market Timings: Meditation Can Work", somebody wrote;

"Though Market Timings has been the key to succeed to some investors, it can be completely unprofitable leading to great loses if proper care is not taken. Depending solely in technical analysis tools will not yield the desired results in your investments. Other factors such as discipline, perseverance, instincts and confidence play an important role in your success in a big way;

I don't know about you, but I start my day with a 15 minutes transcendental meditation which boosts my mood all day long. For many, this will bring positivity all of the day's errands and transactions."

After attending a seminar held by The Center of Leadership Performance, near New York Stock Exchange on Wall Street, Ray Dalio, Head of the Bridgewater Associates, embraced the Transcendental meditation, **"It has increased my employee's clear thinking,"** he said.

"I really want to learn meditation, but I don't know how," said Desire Carroll, a manager at Deloitte who plan to take lessons. Another attendee at the seminar said "everyone doing it, they have a glow and they seem happy."

Mudras

Mudras are the gestures of hand and fingers. The Mudras have curative effects for diseases.

The living body is made up of five elements. They are Fire, Wind, Ether, Earth and Water. Whenever imbalances of these elements occur, the immunity system gets disrupted and diseases are caused. The Mudras help in making up for the deficiencies of these elements by connecting one part of the body with the other.

The five elements are represented by the five fingers as below—

Thumb : Fire

Index Finger : Wind

Middle Finger : Ether

Ring Finger : Earth

Little Finger : Water

When a finger representing an element is brought into contact with the thumb, then the particular element is balanced. The disease caused by the imbalance of that element is cured.

Electromagnetic currents are passed within the body when the tips of the fingers are brought into contact.

You can do these Mudras any time, any place, in bus, train, car, office or at home.

The Mudras should be learned from a Guru and then practiced.

The following are some of the Mudras and their curative effects.

Gyan Mudra

Procedure: Touch the tip of your thumb with the tip of your index finger and keep the remaining fingers absolutely straight.

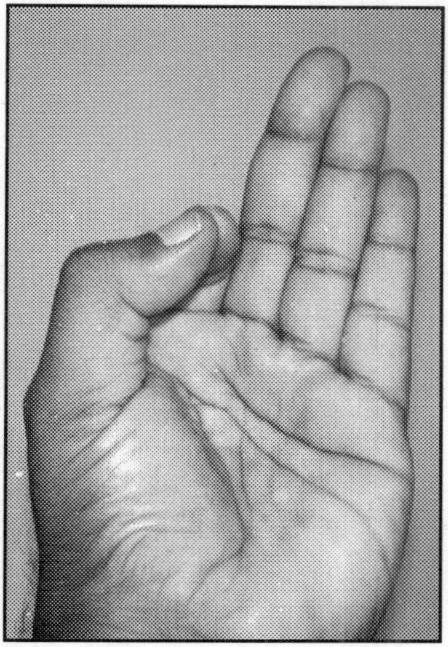

Speciality: As it is a Mudra of knowledge, it enhances the knowledge. The tip of thumb has centers of pituitary and endocrine glands. When we press these centers by index finger the two glands work actively.

Duration: There is no particular time duration for this mudra. You can practice by sitting, standing or lying on bed whenever and wherever you have time

Benefits: It increases memory, intelligence and concentration in studies. Strengthens the nerve system, cures migraines, headache and insomnia, helps in over powering anger and developing spiritualism.

Prithvi Mudra

Procedure: The tips of the thumb and ring finger are placed on top of each other and a light pressure is applied. The other fingers are left extended.

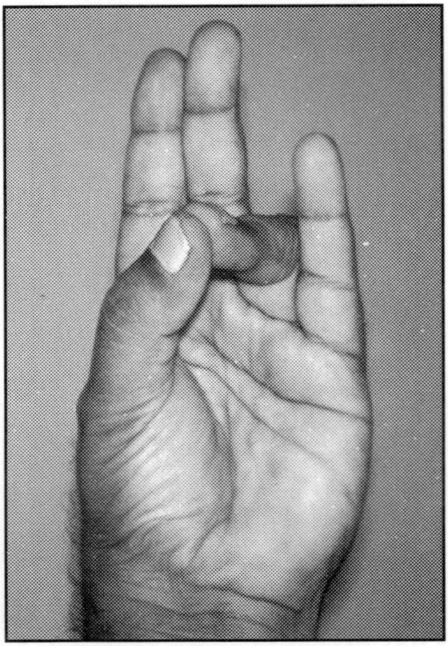

Speciality: This mudra restores the equilibrium and trust of human mind and soul. Prithvi Mudra is recommended for the people who suffer from deficiency of minerals and vitamins and those who have weakness in the body.

Benefits: It helps increase the weight of the weak people. The practice of this mudra removes the fatigue and strengthens the weak or tired organs of the body. it improves skin complexion and makes it glow.

Varuna Mudra

Procedure: This Mudra is formed by joining together the tips of the thumb and the little finger.

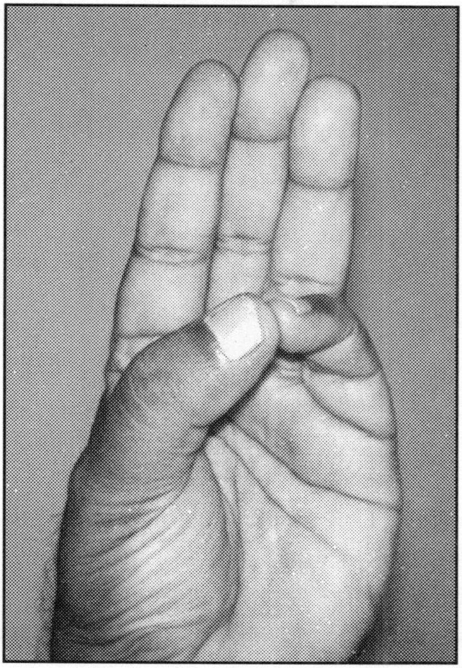

Speciality: It balances the water content and prevents all diseases which occur due to lack of water.

Duration: There is no particular time duration for this Mudra. You can practice by sitting, standing or lying on bed whenever and wherever you have time

Benefits: It retains clarity in blood by balancing water content in the body. It prevents the pains of gastroenteritis and muscle shrinkage. It helps release constipation.

Vayu Mudra

Procedure: The tip of the index finger touches the base of your thumb, and press down the index finger lightly with your thumb, keeping the rest of your fingers straight.

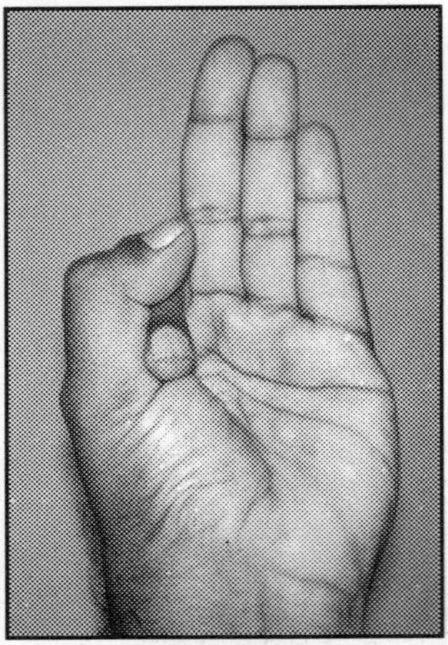

Speciality: This Mudra restores the equilibrium and trust of human mind and soul. Vayu Mudra is recommended for the people who suffer from deficiency of minerals and vitamins and those who have weakness in the body.

Duration: Do not use this Mudra for more than 30 minutes at any point in time. If badly required, it may be done 2-3 times a day for 15 minutes at each time.

Benefits: It gives relief in ailments like arthritis, Ankylosing spondylitis, sciatica, knee pain, cervical spondylosis. For those who experience a lot of gas, after having food, it is good to do this Mudra. This mudra is likely to cure Parkinsons, polio, paralysis. It helps in relieving stiffness in your neck.

Surya Mudra

Procedure: Bend your ring finger towards your palm. Place the length of the thumb over the ring finger. Let the tip of the thumb touches the second knuckle of the ring finger. Straighten the other fingers.

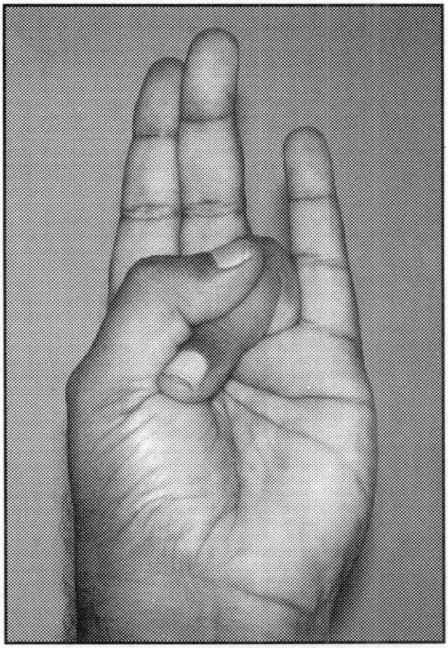

Speciality: It sharpens the center in thyroid gland.

Duration: Practice it daily twice for 5 to 15 minutes.

Benefits: By creating body heat, Sun Mudra lessens the level of cholesterol and reduces your weight. The thyroid gland is sharpened with the regular practice of this Mudra. It is also helpful in curing diabetes and liver disorders. Surya Mudra provides mental calmness and helps get rid of all mental burden.

Prana Mudra

Procedure: Join the tip of the thumb with the tips of little and ring finger. Stretch the other fingers and keep them straight

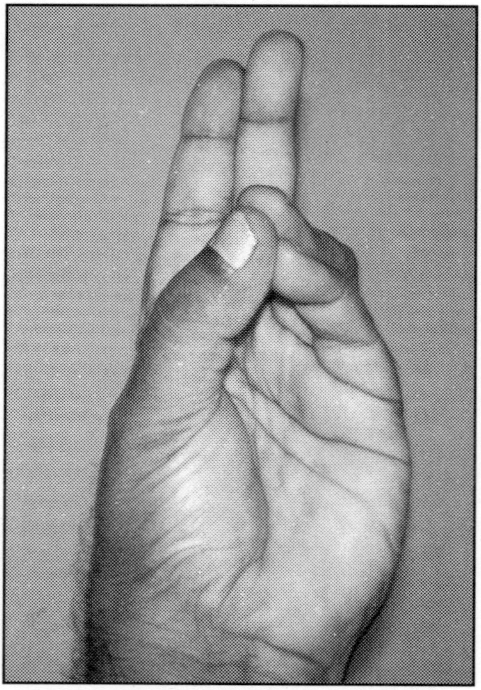

Speciality: As it is the Mudra of life, it improves the power of life. Weak people become strong. It reduces the clamps in blood vessels

Duration: No specific time duration. One can practice it any time.

Benefits: It improves immunity. It improves the power of the eyes and cures eye related diseases. It removes vitamin deficiency and fatigue.

Shunya Mudra

Procedure: Keep the middle finger at the mount of Venus and press it with the thumb.

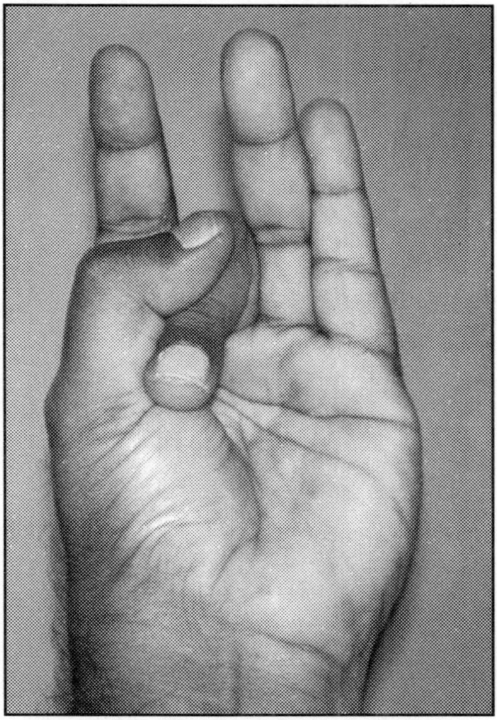

Speciality: It reduces the dullness in our body.

Duration: You can practice it for 40-60 minutes daily until cured.

Benefits: It relieves an earache within 4 or 5 minutes It is useful for the deaf and mentally challenged, but not for inborn ones. Very useful tinnitus (ringing of ears), temporary deafness, weakness of auditory nerves and all other types of ear trouble.

Apan Mudra

Procedure: Join tips of ring fingers, middle fingers and thumb and keep the other two fingers straight. Keep your hands on your folded knees, remember to keep palms facing up. Put a little pressure on joined tips and rest of the hand relaxed.

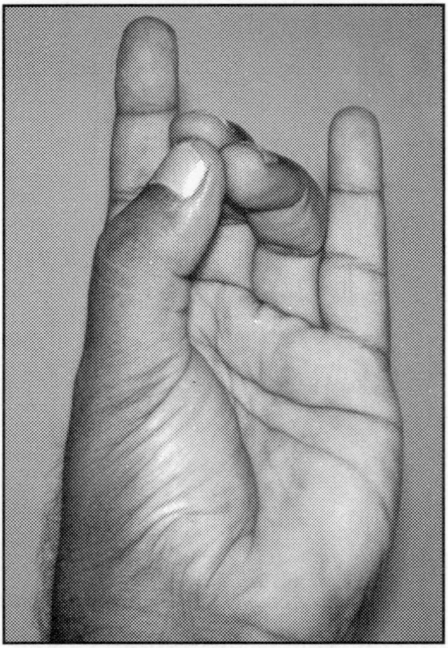

Speciality: Helpful in purification and cleansing of the full body.

Duration: Practice it for 20-30 minutes every day.

Benefits: Helps in purification of the body, urinary problems, easy secretion of excreta, regulating menstruation and painless discharge, easy child delivery, Piles, Diabetes and kidney disorders.

Apana Vayu Mudra

Procedure: Keep the tip of the index finger at the base of the thumb. Join the tips of the thumb, middle and ring fingers. Keep the little finger straight.

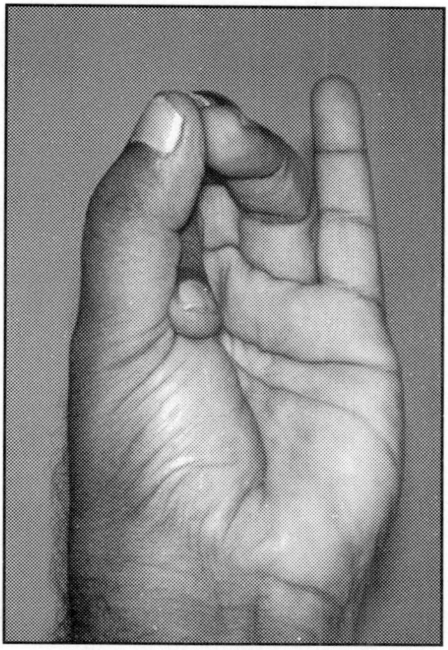

Speciality: This is very useful for Cardiac patients. It is supposed to act as a first aid for heart Problems.

Duration: Practice it as many times as you can. Heart patients and BP patients can practice it for 15 minutes daily twice for better results.

Benefits: In the case of severe heart attack, this is supposed to be a life-giving Mudra. It is supposed to provide instant relief within a few seconds. It regulates the excretory system and redeems gastric trouble.

Ling Mudra

Procedure: Form a fist like figure by crossing/ entangling all the fingers while keeping the thumb of the left hand straight.

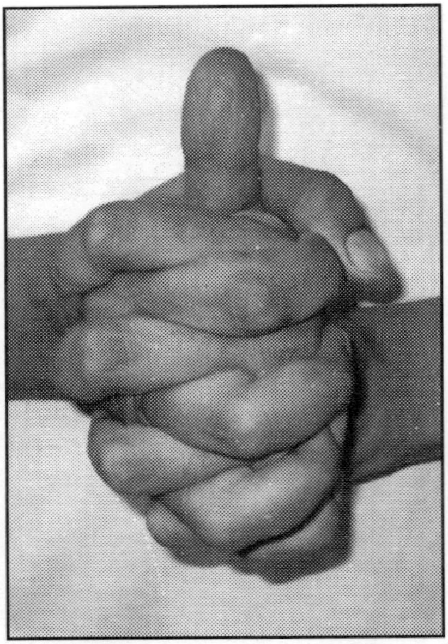

Speciality: It generates heat in our body. Take milk, ghee, more water and fruit juices in addition to practicing this Mudra for improved benefits.

Duration: Practice it any time you want, but do not practice it a lot as it produces heat in the body.

Benefits: It increased body heat and get rid of cough, cold, sinusitis, paralysis and low blood pressure. Care should be taken to take sufficient liquids like water, fruit juice, milk etc. Do not perform this Mudra for too long and if not required.

Regular yoga practice promotes strength, compassion, friendliness, self-awareness and a happy longer life. Further, yoga helps in reducing stress which is the cause of many diseases including cancer and heart disease.

Yoga is an important part of the Indian culture.

Chapter 4

Gandhi and Malaviya

Mahatma Gandhi

Mahatma Gandhi, born on October 2, 1869, was the pre-eminent leader of Indian Nationalism in British-ruled India.

Gandhi was raised in a Hindu community in coastal Gujarat, India. His father, Karamchand Gandhi, a senior officer in the state, was very bold, truthful and a generous man. His mother, Putlibai, was very religious and had strong common sense. She was extremely intelligent and was well informed about all the matters of the state as she worked in the court office. Her saintliness left a deep impression on Gandhi. Gandhi was the youngest of the four children.

Gandhi was very shy at school and avoided all company. He had hard time learning multiplication

tables. Gandhi was very honest from very early at his childhood. In one incidence, at the examination during the first year of high school, an Educational Inspector gave five words to spell in writing. Gandhi misspelt one of the words. The teacher tried to prompt him with the point of his boot for Gandhi to correct it. He wanted him to copy from another student, which Gandhi did not do. The result was that all the boys except him had spelled all the words right. Gandhi did not learn the art of copying.

Gandhi had a long lasting memory of a book about "Shravana" where he devoted his life towards his blind parents carrying them in a hammock for the pilgrimage. One of the photos he saw, where Shravana carrying his parents by means of slings fitted to his shoulders, lasted the impression for the rest of his life.

Another time, he saw a play about "Harishchandra", who was very honest, truthful and dedicated king. **"Why should not all be truthful like Harishchandra"** Gandhi asked himself day and night. Both Shravana and Harishchandara were living realties for Gandhi. Gandhi got married at the age of thirteen to Kasturba.

Gandhi during his childhood

Gandhi got bad company at his early age where he once drank and ate meat. He once stole some money from a family member. He was so ashamed that he decided to write out the confession and give to his father and further asked for forgiveness and for adequate punishment.

He pledged never to do it again. His father was sick and Gandhi gave him this note and sat in the corner. His father read it through, closed his eyes, little drop of water came out of his eyes and tore up the note. Ha had sat up to read it and now he again lay down. Gandhi cried and could not see his agony. Gandhi thought that his father would be very angry but he was very peaceful because of Gandhi's clean confession. He always remembered the kindness and love of his father for the rest of his life. Gandhi's father died a year later.

During the holidays, after first year of the college studies, a family friend visited them and suggested Gandhi to go to England for further studies to become a lawyer. He gave an example of another Lawyer stylishly living after returning from England. His mother was very much worried, so he took an oath not to touch wine, women and meat. His caste-people were agitated of him going abroad as their religion forbade voyages abroad; as they believed it was not possible to live there without meat and wine living with Europeans. As Gandhi insisted on going, an order was pronounced **"this boy should be treated an outcaste from today."** This had no effect on Gandhi and started his

Gandhi in England

journey by sea to England at the age of 18.

In the ship he met an English gentleman who asked him where he was going, what he ate, why he was so shy. As Gandhi told him about his oath of not eating meat and take liquor, the Englishman told Gandhi, "No one to my knowledge, lives there without being a meat eater, I am not asking you to take liquor, but you cannot live without meat." **"I will rather go back to India than eat meat in order to remain there."** Gandhi said.

Gandhi was greeted by friends on his arrival in London. He rented a room and continually thought of his mother, home and his country. All night tears would stream out of his eyes, he could not share the misery with anyone. There was additional inconvenience being vegetarian besides English living. **Even the dishes he could eat were tasteless, but he was determined to finish 3 years of his education in England.**

After returning from England, Gandhi started law practice in India. **On his first case in Bombay for a Defendant, he had to cross-examine the Plaintiff's witness in the court. As he stood up, his heart sank and felt like his head was reeling. He could not think of any question to ask, sat down and told his client that he could not conduct the case, felt ashamed and walked away from the court room.** He left Bombay and started his practice in his hometown, Porbander.

During his practice, he got an opportunity to represent a client in South Africa, so he went there. He found that Indians were not much respected there. In the court, he was asked by the magistrate to remove his turban; Gandhi refused and left the court.

He wrote to the press the incident and got unexpected advertisement in South Africa. The turban stayed with Gandhi throughout his stay in South Africa.

Once, he was traveling in the first class by train to another city in South Africa, he was kicked out of the train for not moving to the third class as non-white person were not allowed to travel in the first class. He sat at the station during cold night and next day he was finally allowed to travel first class to his destination.

In Transvaal, Indians were forced to pay a poll tax of £3 to enter the city. They must not own a property, walk on the side walk and must not move out of the doors after 9 p.m. without a permit. Gandhi often walked past 9 p.m., a man kicked him and pushed to the ground. A person, known to Gandhi, passed by and watched the incidence and offered to be the witness in the court. The incidence was reported to police and the man apologized to Gandhi.

A Bill was being introduced before the House of Legislature which sought to deprive the Indians of their right to elect members of the Natal Legislative Assembly. Gandhi took initiative to prepare and present a petition with ten thousand signatures to the Speaker of the Assembly, opposing the Bill. Copies of this petition were sent to the English and the Indian press. The Times of India and the London Times supported them and the Bill was vetoed out.

In Natal, South Africa, the Indians first came as laborers and later became businessmen and bought many properties. White traders were alarmed and through the politicians, got introduced a bill to impose a tax on indentured Indians, called the poll tax. Gandhi successfully organized a fierce campaign against this tax. Had this Bill would have gone through, it would have been levied and created the problems for Indians for a long time.

Gandhi became famous by fighting for the civil rights of Muslims and Hindu Indians in South Africa, using new techniques of non-violent civil disobedience that he developed. Returning to India, he organized peasants to protest excessive land-taxes.

He became a leader of the Muslims protesting the

declining status of the Caliphate. Assuming leadership of the Indian National Congress in 1921, Gandhi led nationwide campaigns for erasing poverty, expanding women's rights, building religious and ethnic amenity, ending untouchability, increasing economic self-reliance, and much more.

Gandhi led Indians in protesting the National Salt Tax with 400 km (250 mi) Dandi Salt March in

Dandi March

1930, and later demanding the British to immediately Quit India in 1942 during the World War II. He was imprisoned on many occa-sions for political offenses over the years.

Gandhi sought to practice non-violence and truth in all situations, and advocated that others do the same.

He saw the villages as the core of the true India and promoted self- sufficiency. He did not support the industrialization programs of his disciple, Jawaharlal Nehru. He lived modestly in a self-sufficient residential community and wore the traditional Indian dhoti and shawl, woven with yarn he had hand spun on a charkha (spinning wheel). Gandhi's chief political enemy in Britain was Winston Churchill, who ridiculed him as a "half-naked fakir." He was a dedicated vegetarian, and undertook long fasts as means of both self-purification and political mobilization.

The Swadeshi movement, a part of the Indian independence movement and developing the Indian

Gandhi and other Indian Leaders

nationalism, were an economic strategy aimed at removing the British Empire from the power and improving economic conditions in India by following the principles of Swadeshi (self-sufficiency), which had some success. Strategies of the Swadeshi movement involved boy-cotting British products and the revival of domestic products and the production processes.

Gandhi achieved success in getting Swaraj, the independence of India, from Britain in 1947.

On January 30, 1948 Gandhi was walking on the

Gandhi Funeral Procession

steps of a temple in Delhi for prayer meeting when he was shot dead. Millions of people attended the funeral of Gandhi. Gandhi is regarded as the "Father of the Nation."

Pt. Nehru, the ex-Prime Minister of India said about Gandhi, "He lives in the hearts of millions of people and

Jawaharlal Nehru

he will live for immortal ages. In time to come, people will think of this man of divine fire and follow his path."

Martin Luther King

Martin Luther King said, "we may ignore Gandhi at our own risk."

Lord Mountbatten said, "Gandhi's death is truly a loss to mankind which sorely needs the living light of those ideals of love and tolerance for which he strived and died."

Madan Mohan Malaviya

Madan Mohan Malaviyaji

Madan Mohan Malaviya was a visionary of modern India as described by Dr. S.K. Maini in his book, 'Madan Mohan Malaviya' which was launched by the Prime Minister of India, Dr. Manmohan Singh, in December of 2011 at Delhi.

Gandhiji said "I am devotee of Malaviyaji. I do not consider anyone a greater patriot than Malaviyaji. I always worship him."

Mr. Malaviya (Malaviyaji, as he was respectfully called) was born in 1861, was among 8 children. His father was very learned and respected person. His mother, Moona Devi was a very devoted and a religious person.

Malaviyaji's early years were spent in a small ancestral house which was shared by his father and four uncles. He went to school in Allahabad. Even after his entry into modern education, he privately studied Bhagavd Gita and the scriptures. In December 1883, he received his B.A. examination at Calcutta University. He was a voracious reader and with sharp memory and intellect. He started working as a teacher at a high school in 1885.

Madan Mohan Malviyaji and Gandhi

Malaviyaji got married to Kundan Devi at the age of 16. They had 12 children out of which 7 survived.

Right from his formative years, Malavyiji exhibited the unique chacteristics of taking usually bold initiatives and quick decisions and then executing them effectively and with poise. The first major leap in his life came when his teacher, Pandit Aditya Ram Bhattacharya, took him along to attend the second Congressional Session held in Calcutta. There Malaviyaji gave a very impressive speech and was received very enthusiastically by the Congress leaders. Again in 1987, Malaviyaji spoke on the necessity of the reform at the Congress session, Dr. Maini wrote in his book.

He started as a journalist in 1980 and later started his own newspaper, The Leader, an English Daily.

Malaviyaji studied law and started his practice in 1891. He rose to eminence in his profession among other advocates of his time like Pt. Moti Lal Nehru. In addition, judges openly commended Malaviyaji.

Gandhi, Malviyaji and Radhakrishnan

Gandhiji said "Even today, leaving his law practice of more than a lakh of monthly income, he is ceaselessly involved in the service of the country."

After retirement Malaviyaji appeared in the court only twice. In Chauri Chaura Case of 1922, 170 persons were sentenced to death for burning a police station, where 22 policemen were burnt alive. Malaviyaji saved 151 of them from the jaws of death.

In 1909, Malaviyaji got elected to the prestigious position of the Congress President. Malaviyiji was acknowledged as the top leader in 1917. Gandhi and Nehru and others wished to be with him for the success of any programme. He got elected Congress President again in 1918, 1932 and in 1933.

Malaviyaji's ideology included the winning of freedom through inter-communal harmony with mutual trust. He said "we will have to make such a law and such a constitution that no body may be afraid of anyone else in the country in whatever circumstances he be placed."

Malaviyaji sacrificed his practice for managing Banaras Hindu University.

Banaras Hindu University

In 1906, Malaviyaji started campaign of starting Banaras Hindu University (BHU). A site of 1300 acres was secured. A great campaign was launched to raise the funds. A sum of 151 lakhs was raised and foundation stone for the university was laid in 1916. The first college started working at the University was College of Arts (1917). **Dr. Maini was also a student of BHU and further received an Honorary Doctorate in Technology from the very respectable Loughborough University, England. Dr. Radhakrishnan, ex-President of India, was also the Vice Chancellor of BHU. Its alumni have occupied very important and respected posts such as that of the President, Prime Minister and the Chief of the Supreme Court, on top of many CEO's of large companies. BHU ranked number one university from 1993-2002 in India.**

The Twelfth Annual Convocation was held in 1929 and convocation address was delivered by Malaviyaji, exhorting them he said: ''you must always be prepared to do the duty that your country may demand of you, love your countrymen and promote unity among them. I call upon every one of you, young men and women, to take a vow that you will start a crusade against illiteracy, a campaign to spread knowledge and enlightenment among the teaming millions of Indians,'' Dr. Maini wrote in his book.

Social Work started from the very beginning of Malaviyaji's life when, as a youth in 1989, he founded Bharatiya Bhavan Library which is serving even today the citizens of Allahabad. Malaviyaji's was very keen on educating the depressed class and the poor.

Malaviyaji defined Righteous Living or Sanatana Dharma as the integration of all the right human values. He firmly believed that these values could be practiced only when they are inculcated as an inseparable part of each individual's character.

Another area which Malaviyaji stressed was 'discipline' in the life of a student. He often used to say that every work will be successful when student observe celibacy, concentrate on studies, drink plenty of milk, play and exercise well, pray to God and work with full confidence.

Malaviyaji died on November12, 1946 in Varanasi. The whole nation was plunged in grief as thoughts part of India's heart had been lost forever. Thousands of people thrust forward to have a last glimpse of the mortal remains of the great soul and there was a three-mile long queue of mourners.

Gandhiji said ''Malaviya is immortal. Like the King of England whose death was proclaimed by the forms, the King is dead; Long live King; it may be said of Malaviyaji, whom death has kindly delivered from physical pain, Malaviya the adore of Bharatavarsha is dead, long live Malaviyaji.'' (From the book ''Madan Mohan Malaviya'' written by Dr. S.K.Maini).

Dr. S. K. Maini

Gandhi and Malviya are the pillars of the Indian Culture.

•

Chapter 5

Taj Mahal

President Clinton's daughter, Chelsea, visited the Taj Mahal in 1995 with her mother, Hillary Clinton, and said, **"when I was little, this was sort of embodiment of the Fairy-Tale palace to me."** Chelsea said while visiting Taj Mahal.

"I would see pictures of it and would dream I was a princess or whatever. Now that I am here, it is spectacular," Chelsea said.

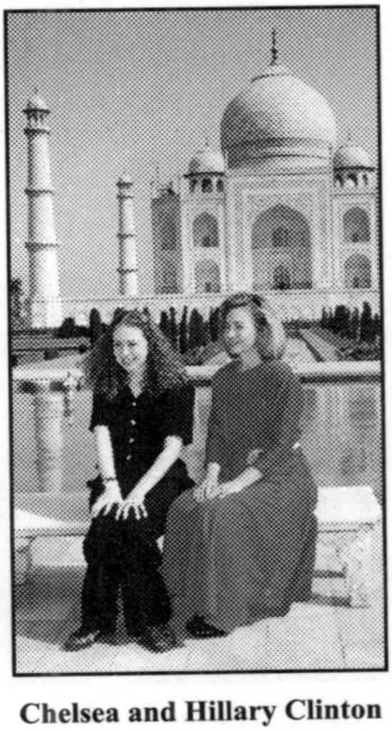

Chelsea and Hillary Clinton

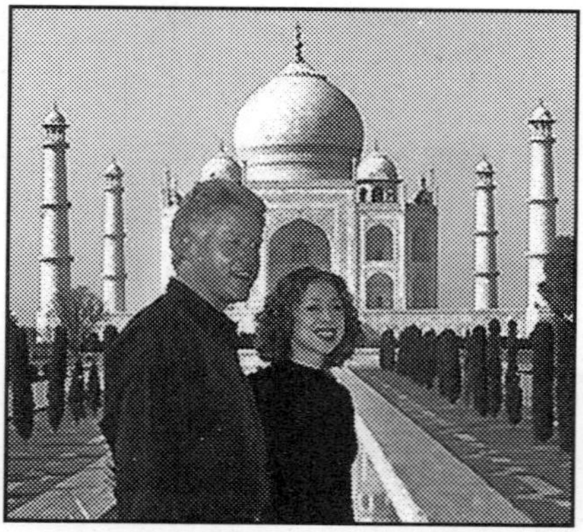

Bill and Chelsea Clinton

During the Canadian Prime Minister's visit to Taj Mahal with his wife in 2013, **he was asked if he was planning anything similar for his wife.** The question prompted laughter from the Prime Minister and Laureen Harper, who was standing at his side.

"My wife has taste a little more modest," said Mr. Harper, as he smiled. **"And she also wants them while she's still living."** Laureen Harper, also grinning, added her own comment: "I'm not waiting until I'm dead."

Canadian Prime Minister Harper and his wife

Asked why he chose to make this his first stop, Harper had a direct answer, **"It's iconic,"** he said. **"This is the thing, and believe**

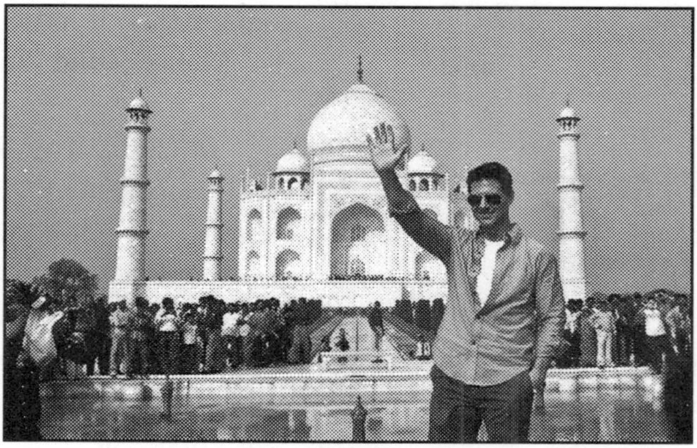

Tom Cruise

me, it's worth seeing. I recommend it to anyone."

Most of the dignitaries, who visit India, also make it a point to see Taj Mahal. When I first visited Taj, I was stunned to see the pure white structure shinning in the sunlight. This was the most beautiful thing I had ever seen. All over the world, Taj Mahal's name and photos are being used on many famous hotels and by many businesses. We have heard very famous and historical

Oprah Winfrey

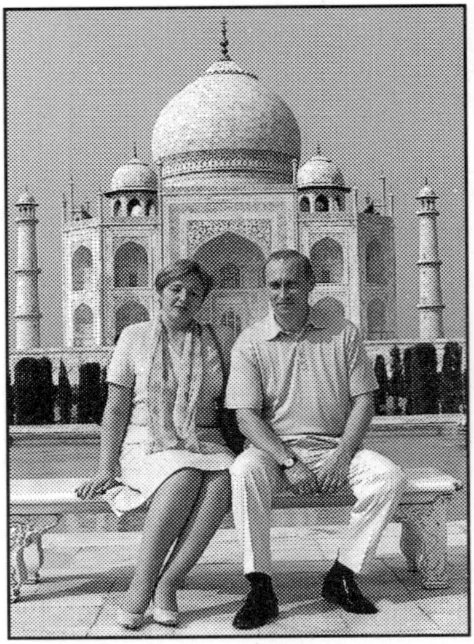

Russian President Putin and his wife

monuments of India, but Taj Mahal is the unique one.

In 2002, I noticed an advertisement in a major Canadian newspaper, about the world's tallest tower, CN Tower, in Toronto. What drew my attention was that on this full page ad, they showed full picture of Taj Mahal with 4 pillars, but one of the front pillar (right) they replaced it with their 'CN Tower'. In the middle of this page they wrote only one line in bold,

President of China Hu Jintao and his wife

Indian actress Aishwarya Rai

saying: **"show them our place in the world, CN Tower".**

Later, I noticed another full page ad, showing large picture of Taj Mahal, in another national newspaper. This ad was about promoting a Visa credit card by a major Canadian Bank showing that the card holder can get a free ticket to go and see world's most beautiful monument by using the credit card and accumulating the bonus points.

Taj Mahal is the most famous name in the world.

Love Story

Taj Mahal is one of the most beautiful love story engraved in white marble, an inspiration for many lovers, poets, actors, film producers for its irresistible beauty.

Prince Shah Jahan, son of King Jahangir, was a very handsome young man. **One day, he went to bazaar and**

noticed a very beautiful young girl, Mumtaz, selling glass mirrors and beads. He bought some mirrors and kept her images in his mind. He was very young at that time. As the Prince grew up, he wanted to marry his love of his life, Mumtaz. But King's wife wanted Shah Jahan to marry her daughter from the previous marriage. Upon refusal, King's wife sent her secret force to kill Mumtaz. She also persuaded the King, to send forces to fight Shah Jahan, who was gone to another province with Mumtaz on a battle field.

Shah Jahan fought back and declared that Mumtaz was superior to him than the Mugal Dynasty and that he would sacrifice the Kingdom. On seeing the conflict, Mumtaz persuaded Shah Jahan to make peace with the King and marry his father's choice of an Iranian girl. Queen's daughter finally married Shah Jahan's brother. Later, Shah Jahan also married Mumtaz. Shah Jahan had three wives but Mumtaz was his favorite. Mumtaz was a year younger than him.

The love story of this young couple is the basis of the Taj Mahal.

After the King died, Shah Jahan became the Ruler. Both were very happy. Mumtaz always accompanied Shah Jahan on his various war trips. In one of her trips, she got sick during her fourteenth childbirth. Soon after giving birth to a daughter, she became very week and died at the age of 39.

Shah Jahan was so devastated that he stopped any celebration and music in the country for two years. It is said that Shah Jahan died in spirit, the day his Queen Mumtaz died. Stories are told of, how he shut himself up in a room after her death and when he came out next morning his hair had turned white.

Before dying, Mumtaz made Shah Jahan to promise four things, one of which was to build a memorial for their undying love and for him to visit the memorial every year on her death anniversary.

Shah Jahan, in order to perpetuate the memory of his favorite wife, Mumtaz Mahal, who died in 1631, had this funerary mosque built. Shah Jahan was a passionate architect. He hired the best architects of the world and picked up the best material. The monument, begun in 1632, unverified but nonetheless, tenacious, legends attribute its construction to an international team of several thousands of masons, marble workers, mosaicists and decorators.

Taj Mahal, an immense mausoleum of white marble, is the jewel of Muslim art in India and one of the universally admired masterpieces of the world's heritage. It no doubt partially owes its renown to the moving circumstances of its construction.

Situated on the right bank of the Yamuna in a vast Mogul garden of some 35 acres, this funerary monument, bounded by four isolated minarets, reigns with its octagonal structure capped by a bulbous dome through the crisscross of open perspectives offered by alleys or basins of water.

The materials were brought in from all over India and central Asia and white Makrana marble from Jodhpur. Precious stones for the inlay came from Baghdad, Punjab, Egypt, Russia, Golconda, China, Afghanistan, Ceylon, Indian Ocean and Persia. The unique Mughal style combines elements and styles of Persian, Central Asian and Islamic architecture.

Taj Mahal is a large three-storey structure. It was completed in 1648, with an octagonal central chamber with a vaulted roof and with smaller rooms on each side. The gateway consists of lofty central arch with two-storied wings on either side. The walls are inscribed with verses from the Qur'an in Arabic in black calligraphy. The small domed pavilions on top are Hindu in style and signify royalty. The gate was originally lined with silver, now replaced with copper.

The ornamental gardens, through which the paths lead, are planned along classical Mughal Char Bagh style. Two marble canals studded with fountains, lined with cypress trees emanating from the central, raised pool cross in the centre of the garden, dividing it into four equal squares. In each square there are 16 flower beds, making a total of 64 with around 400 plants in each bed. The feature to be noted is that the garden is laid out in such a way as to maintain perfect symmetry. The channels, with a perfect reflection of the Taj, used to be stocked with colorful fish and the gardens with beautiful birds.

The Taj Mahal itself, situated in the north end of the garden, stands on two bases, one of sandstone and above it a square platform worked into a black and white checker board design and topped by a huge blue-veined white marble terrace, on each corner there are four minarets. On the east and west sides of the tomb are identical red sandstone buildings. On the west is the masjid (mosque), which sanctifies the area and provides a place of worship. On the other side is the jawab, which cannot be used for prayer as it faces away from Mecca. The roza, the central structure or the mausoleum on the platform, is square with beveled corners. Each corner has small domes while in the centre is the main double dome topped by a brass finial.

The main chamber inside is octagonal with a high domed ceiling. This chamber contains false tombs of Mumtaz and Shah Jahan, laid to rest in precise duplicates. Both tombs are exquisitely inlaid and decorated with precious stones, the finest in Agra.

Shah Jahan had four sons who grew up in an atmosphere of bitter rivalry. In 1657, Shah Jahan became seriously ill. The expectation of an early death provoked the four sons into making a desperate bid for the throne.

One of his sons, Aurangzeb was well educated, knowledgeable in the traditional spectrum of Islamic studies, and strict in his religious orthodoxy. Aurangzeb had an acute sense of political realism and a fierce appetite for power. Although Aurangzeb's personality was considered less attractive than other sons but he was superior in both military talent and administrative skills.

Aurangzeb easily outclassed his brothers in the bid for power. During his 30-year reign, Shah Jahan had never expected that his last days would be so utterly tragic. With his old age and his poor health, Shah Jahan could only helplessly watch the serious outbreak of hostility among his sons. Shah Jahan was a mere spectator at the savage contest. **The emergence of Aurangzeb as the undisputed victor led to the father's imprisonment in the Agra fort.**

Shah Jahan was confined to the fort for eight years.

According to legend, when Shah Jahan was on his death-bed, he kept his eyes fixed on the Taj Mahal which was clearly visible from his place of confinement. He died in 1666 and was buried quietly next to the cenotaph of Mumtaz in Taj Mahal.

Taj Mahal represents the Indian Culture.

●

Chapter 6

Corruption

Jackie Chan, the famous Action Movie Star, stated in an interview with Phoenix TV that **"America is the most corrupt country in the world."**

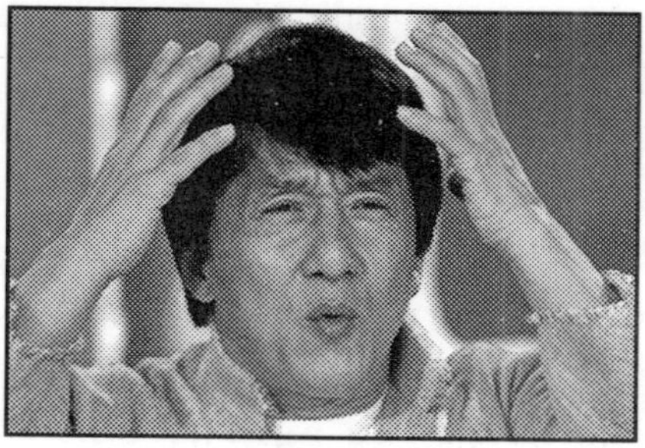

Jackie Chan

Corruption is common all over the world and America is not immune to it either. There are more than one million lawyers to handle the corrupt, criminals and others in the United States. **Its jails are full with about 3,000,000 people while in India, about 350,000 people are in jails.**

Corruption is defined as 'on the part of an authority or powerful party that acts illegitimate, immoral or incompatible with ethical standard. Corruption may include activities like bribery or government employee acts in an official capacity for personal gain. Improper and unlawful conduct intended to secure a benefit for oneself or others is corruption.'

In a blog, one person wrote, ''There is plenty of corruption in America and that US is very corrupt."

Another person wrote, "If US was not corrupt, then why is that when Ted Kennedy kills a women while driving, he does not spend a day in jail. Robert Downey Jr. keeps getting arrested for drugs, yet he keeps getting out. If I was doing the same thing, I will be in jail. I always say that in capital countries, the rich never go to jail for their crime." He further said "if you talk to some people from the military industry complex, then you can see how the USA actually is."

Jonathan...wrote "I agree that America is the most corrupt country on the world on mass scale..."

Dan wrote, "honestly, Jackie Chan is pretty much spot on. The US is horribly corrupt and won't admit it, just sweep it under the rug and pretend it does not exist..."

Dr. Leslie Sachs, an author, journalist and an expert in US corruption with 7 degrees including two from Harvard, said that United States is the largest prison gulag in the world - 25% of all the prisoners in the entire world. In his book, "The Virginia Ghost Murders," a very popular novel book of good old boys corruption of Virginia Society and Government, he said that "We have prisoners 30 times higher than China."

Pensions

Pension is defined as an allowance, annuity or subsidy. Pension is also defined as a fixed amount, other than wages paid in regular intervals to a person in consideration of past service.

President Roosevelt

In 1935, President Roosevelt created Pensions. In 1953, President Eisenhower created Health, Education and Welfare. In 1995, President Clinton made SSA, Social Security Agency as an independent agency. Lately, the pensions have been misused by many individuals and by various organizations, have become a part of corruption in America.

The Pensions are a big problem in America. Recently, Detroit is the largest city, ever declared bankruptcy in USA, largely due to lack of funding of employees pensions. According to NY Times, CNN and other news agencies, many other cities face the similar problems. The greed has taken over in pensions.

In a blog, Bill wrote—"All over the United States, public employees and teachers secure enormous salaries and pensions that private sector cannot afford. Public sector and economy has become the servant of government workers, we need real public non-union servants that work hard to taxpayer at the affordable wages and benefits not extortion Artists like we have now."

Another person wrote, "Time to take money away from responsible upstanding citizens and give to the irresponsible to pay their bills, we now live on a country where it pays to be a dead beat."

Alec wrote, "We can take America back from the rest of the world by standing our grounds against corruption."

I was listening to a radio talk show where a man was commenting on an accident, where a 14 years old girl was killed by a truck while crossing the road, just across the school. He blamed that death on the teachers and their unions for taking huge amount of school budgets for their salaries, pensions and benefits and leaving short of funds for safety and other issues concerning children.

This is happening all over USA. Maintenance of the buildings, library closings or other students activities are being compromised because of funding being diverted to teachers, pensions and benefits. In one school Board in Michigan, these benefits increased from 13% of the payroll budget to 27%, in just 10 years. Similar situation happened in Chicago School Board and other places. It is estimated that in a few years these pensions will be under funded on the magnitude of 2.5 trillion dollars

In Chicago, more than 80 ex-police officers have pensions over $100,000 a year, according to Taxpayers United of America. Police and firefighter's pensions are $55,000-$70,000. In California, more than 14,000 retired public employees draw pension of more than $100,000 a year. Many of these retired persons also receive thousands of dollars of federal social security benefits every year. Some also earn through other jobs, earning extra money as they retire after 30 years of service in their fifties.

In a social gathering, I heard a conversation where an ex-government employee described, how

employees have ripped off the municipalities by increasing their last five years of income for the purposes of increasing their pensions.

The way it works, as explained by that ex-employee, that many union contracts call for pension to be calculated based on average income earned during last 3 or 5 years. You get 2% of your salary multiplied by the number of years worked. For example, if your salary is $100,000 a year and if you have been able to increase the salary, by receiving overtime from other employees to $150,000 a year for 3-5 years and worked 30 years before retirement, you will receive 2% of 150,000 which is 3,000 multiply by 30. You will receive $90,000 a year for rest of your life, which is much more than normal $60,000/year which you would have received based on $100,000 salary. This amount could be in hundreds of millions of dollars in larger cities. This is done with the help of other employees who pass their over time to this retiring employee in order to show his higher income to qualify for higher pensions, and in turn they get themselves the same, when their time for the retirement comes.

In a small town Bell, in the state of California with a population of under 40,000, a big scandal took place in the years of around 2008-2010. The Mayor, Council members Police Chief and others increased their salaries and pensions up to 10 times than normal.

The Mayor's salary was increased to about $440,000 while council members to $100,000. Police chief received $350,000. There was a Police force of only 48 officers in town. In Los Angeles, with a police force of 10,000 persons, Police Chief was paid a salary of $350,000. The President of the United States receives a salary of $400,000 while the Mayor of this small town, Bell, was receiving a salary of $440,000.

This is how the corruption is being manipulated by some of the public employees. Poor citizens end up holding the bag for long time.

Restaurant in Michigan

I was sitting in a restaurant in Michigan, when a younger person walked in to give ride to a retired person, loudly asking him to rush up. And further he yelled to the retired person, "people like you have exhausted funds for our pensions in the future." This is so true. At the end of the day, public pay the price in higher property taxes or lowers in the services.

I compared property tax of a house in an American city comparable to a Canadian city; it was almost double in USA. That is the cost of corruption to American people while these retirees taking cruises or gambling in casinos.

Governors and Mayors in Jail

In the last few years, many politicians including Governors, Mayors, Senators, Congressmen, Police Chiefs and even Judges have been jailed for corruption in USA.

4 out of previous 7 Illinois (Chicago) governors went to prison

Clockwise from left:
Otto Kerner, George Ryan, Rod Blagojevich, Dan Walker

In one state, Illinois (capital, Chicago), out of last 7 Governors, four (Blagojevich, Ryan, Walker, Kerner) were convicted of corruption and sent to jail. There are 50 states in USA.

Mayors from many States including from New Jersey (12 Mayors), California (3), Illinois (3), Alabama (3), Florida (2), Michigan (1) and so on, were convicted and many were sent to jail.

Police Corruption

The police are so corrupt that their public trust has dropped to about 25% from 80%, just in a few years. Police lies all over because in the courts, judges trust Police more than the public. Police has taken advantage of the situation and now more and more evidence has come out. There are no action against police if they lie in court even it is proven a perjury, prosecutors do not take actions against them. Police is involved in all kinds of crimes including alcohol and drug smuggling, drinking at job, stealing from people, storage and even from dead men, forging and preparing fake documents to falsely convicting people. Police are the most corrupt people in the country. This has caused billions of dollars of losses to the government in terms of time, lawsuits, work losess and others.

Ex-Romulus Police Chief (Michigan), Michael St. Andre and 5 other faced trial in September of 2012 for Corruption.

Ex-Police Chief of Chicago, Regina Evans, was charged in April 2012 for corruption charges.

3 former Wayne County employees including treasurer and a school official charged in 2012 for corruption. In this county, many officials were charged with extortion and fraud.

Courthouse Corruption

Now even Courthouse corruption came in the picture which involved a Crown Attorney. Of a corruption scandal in the justice system, a senior provincial police officer, Rutigliano who was a court case management officer, found himself in the wrong side of the law. In a sexual assault charges against D'Angelo, who was acquitted, Mr. Rutigliano was charged with obstruction of justice and 2 crown attorneys were removed from active duty. Mr. Rutigliano also faced eight other charges, including allegations that he and three other co-accused tried to defraud Bombardier Inc. of $15 million in a purported kickback and secret commission's scheme.

Judges in Jail

In 2013, Michigan Supreme court Justice Diane Hathaway was sentenced to one year in jail for fraud.

FORMER JUSTICE DIANE HATHAWAY
SENTENCED TO 1 YEAR IN PRISON

She fraudulently transferred one of her property in order to hide her assets declaring that she did not had any assets to pay loans for her other property. She was charged for bank fraud and money laundering by the U.S. Prosecutors, according to Chad Livengood of Detroit news.

Stack of $100 Bills

Fire Chief of Godmanchester, Que., Andrew McDonald and 3 other firefighters were among 22 people arrested in smuggling Tobacco.

In an inquiry in Montreal, 2 Municipal employees, that they have accepted a variety of gifts from construction companies. Mr. Leclare, one of the municipal employees said, "How openly the civil servants accepted favors, wine meals, round of golf, hockey tickets etc." He was astounded then quickly fell in line, "While in Rome, do as the Romans do" he explained. He estimated over 20 years, he accepted about $500,000 plus countless gifts. "At first I refused categorically, saying it was out of question to have my hands tied and I do not want to owe anything to a contractor," he testified **"But the evening wore on, the wine flowed and Mr. Catania proved persuasive, at the end of the meal, I said yes." Two years later, another contractor slipped him a Christmas card over a dinner containing a "beautiful $1000 bill." Again he hesitated, he said, but again he kept it.**

An employee, a city engineer, Mr. Surprenant testified that he took $700,000 before retiring. They over billed the City, for construction firms, for projects and for extras, where the work was not performed. Mr. Surprenant testified that another superior, **Yves Themens in his office, once called him in his office to show him a stack of $100 bills that he said had come from "Tony", a contractor.**

In Quebec, a contractor testified in the inquiry that he received Mafia death threat. He received a pink condolence card with written message, "Dear Friend, stop bidding in Montreal. If not, your family will get a card just like this one. FINAL WARNING."

A CEO of a large company, Pierre Duhaime, with

more than One billion dollar contract in Montreal was arrested and charged with fraud and forged documents for missing $56 million.

Black market is so common that people are working on cash without any receipts, paying no sales taxes, excise taxes and income taxes. On the top of that they are under bidding the regular honest business people and ruining their business with the result that these companies are closing businesses.

Charity Corruption

Charity has been defined as the generous actions or donations to aid the poor, ill or helpless or to devote one's life to charity.

In America, many charitable organizations have ripped off the public to the unbelievable amount. Recently I watched a program on CNN's Anderson Cooper's AC 360, where they showed that **America's 50 worst Charities collected about $1.3 billion in donations, out of which about 3% actual used to benefit the needy. That means over $1.2 billion used for fees and personal benefits.**

One charity in Florida, Kids Wish Network collected $127.8 million in 10 years period, in the name of dying children and their families, but spent less than $4 million on direct cash aid.

They lied to the donors by taking multiple salaries and secretly paid themselves as consulting fees.

In Tennessee, youth Development Fund raised $30 million in last decades and paid 80% to solicitors to raise funds. Most of whatever left, spent on things like Scuba Diving Video, starring the Founder and President, Rick Brown's own video and profit company paying himself $200,000 to make video. It claims that it reaches 1.2 million audiences. According to Station Manager, radio show attracted only 3,000. The President ran this charity from his own condo.

Most of the larger charities are spending about half or less on needy people. According to David Emery (About.com),

March of Dimes spend 1 dime to a dollar for needy

Red Cross spend 39 cents for every dollar on needy. President of Red Cross receives $650,000 + benefits. On top she gets 6 weeks paid holidays.

United Way spend 51 cents on needy for every dollar received. President receives $375,000 + benefits.

Goodwill spend 5 cents on every dollar for needy. The President of Goodwill receives $2.7 million in compensation.

UNICEF 51 cents of every dollar goes to needy. President receives $1.2 million + benefits + Rolls Royce to drive.

unicef

Salvation Army spends 93 cents of every dollar it collects. The President gets less than $200.000 + housing.

Wall Street Corruption

New York Stock Exchange

World's largest and busiest stock exchange is located on the Wall Street, New York. This is world's center of largest Corporations, Banks and Hedge Funds. This is the Head Office of many of the largest Investment Bankers and Stock Brokers of the world. Millions of people are employed in financial related fields in New York.

This is also the center of the greed of the world. In 1986, in a speech at the University of California, Berkeley, a well known Wall Street Ichon, Ivon Boesky, said that "greed is healthy." In 1987, a film

Ivon Boesky

Michael Milken

was made by Oliver Stone where Gordon Gekko (played by Michael Douglas) made a speech "Greed is...good." This film was made on a true story of a stock broker, Michael Milken, who made more than $600 million in inside trading and was sent to jail for long time.

Michael Douglas in the Movie "WALL STREET"

Adam Smith, the godfather of free market capitalism, once said this: "The disposition to admire and almost worship the rich and the powerful is the great and most universal cause of the corruption of our moral sentiments."

This greed caused the financial meltdown of the Wall Street and the housing market.

''Most financial scandals are the reasons of the failure of the rules, or the moral values, that over rule greed. When there is unconstrained greed for profit, then we get the corporate governance meltdown of 2001, the financial crisis of 2008," Judge Rakoff's criticism of the Securities Exchange Commission settlements with Citigroup and Bank of America, whose securities made them hundreds of millions of dollars but lost even more for their clients.

This kind of greed earned Wall Street, a confidence-in-leadership ranking lower than that of Congress, the news media and the White House.

Goldman Sachs and the Street then and through to the days of Lloyd Blankfein have always insisted that they are merely adhering to the iron law of marketplace competition and the relentless discipline of the bottom line, which they are always ready to point out, in the end benefits us all. It is

Llyod Blankfein

fruitless to expect the financial community to voluntarily impose a moral discipline on itself.

In 1951, stock exchange volume averaged 1.8 million shares per day; now it's a rare day when less than 5 billion shares are traded. As small financial firms became giants, a whole new culture started brewing. A professional culture evolved into a business culture.

Trading costs and management fees divert an ever larger proportion of wealth from clients, reducing their share of the returns earned by stocks and bonds. From 1970 to 2007, the trading costs and management fees have increased from 6% to 35% of the earning of S & P 500.

Whenever there were regulations imposed, Wall Street always opposed. Even after the crash of 1929, Richard Whitney, the President of the New York Stock Exchange, responded to investigators, **"you gentlemen are making a great mistake. This exchange is a perfect institution."**

In the crises of financial meltdown of 2007, major cause was the Wall Street, where they bundled large pools of mortgage based securities and sold on the Wall Street for their fees and commissions. Banks were loaning the customer up to 100% or even higher than the values of their homes and other properties. The income and assets of the applicants were not thoroughly verified. All the mortgage brokers, bank officials, Wall Street companies were making millions of dollars as fees. Every one closed their eyes to make money for themselves, which was greed of the highest magnitude by its definition.

The values of the houses started dropping all over the United States 1n 2006-2007, banks started tumbling and auto companies started shutting down their plants.

Auto sales dropped from over 17 million cars at peak time to nearly half to about 9 million cars per year by 2009. There were layoffs in almost every plant of GM, Ford and Chrysler. The auto related companies, dealerships were going bankrupt, retail stores, restaurants started closing down. **The unemployment rate went up from below 5% to 10% in short period of time. As people did not have money, they start defaulting on the loans on their houses.** Most people have bought with little or no down payments, walked away from their homes leaving banks with huge inventories. There were many states which were hardest hit including, Nevada, Florida, California, Michigan, Arizona etc. where property values dropped 50% or more.

Default on the loans reached to such an epidemic that world's largest banks and financial institutions were shaken to their roots. Banks which started more than 50 years ago, were brought to shame to their founders when they were shut down or forced to merge with others, losing their identities. Their equities eroded as much as 90% of their values from the peak.

Their capital eroded with the crash of Wall Street. There were many days in 2007-2008, when the Dow Jones Index dropped as much as 5%, losing hundreds of billions of dollars in a single day. The Index dropped to nearly 7000, losing almost 50% of the value from just couple of years earlier.

Auto companies ran out of cash. They could not pay their day today expenses and ran to Congress begging for money. In the Congressional hearing, when CEO's of GM, Ford and Chrysler were rebuked by congressmen that these executives came in private jets with a tin cup in their hands. This brought such a shame to these executives that they drove to Washington for the next congressional hearing.

The stocks of auto and related companies lost equities by more than 90% of their values from the peak time. There was fear that United States will lose auto manufacturing business, like textile, furnishing and others as in the previous years. There were millions of jobs in danger of losing. Congress and President rushed to save them.

U.S. Attorney of Southern District of New York, Mr. Bharara, cracked down inside trading against 3 hedge fund portfolio managers and a hedge fund analyst in which they conspired to earn more than 30 million dollars. In 2011 they pleaded guilty and sentenced to jail.

Raja Rajaratnam

In 2011, Mr. Bharara got the kingpin of 7 billion dollar Galleon Group hedge fund manager, Raja Rajaratnam (a onetime billionaire), convicted on 14 counts of Inside trading. He was sentenced to jail for many years and fined for millions of dollars. Mr. Bharara further charged 26 former traders, executives and lawyers which he called the biggest probe of inside trading in the $1.9 trillion hedge fund industry. Rajaratnam was accused of making millions of dollars in illegal profit.

Goldman's shares were among 35 stocks cited in the charges. Goldman was not accused of wrong doing. Lloyed Blankfein, CEO of Goldman Sachs Group, also testified in Rajaratnam the largest case of inside trading of 276 million dollar, Mathew Martoma, 38, was arrested for allegedly helping the hedge fund, SAC Capital Advisors benefited from what may be called the most lucrative inside tip of all the time. Preet Bharara said that this was the largest scandal discovered since the crackdown and of more than 70 arrests in inside trading system began.

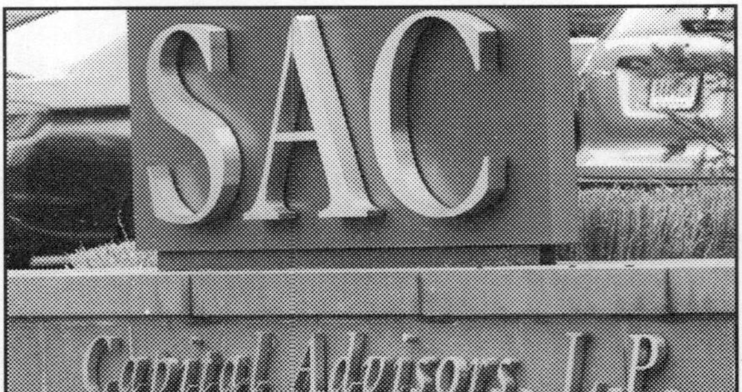

In 2013, SAC Capital was fined 1.8 billion dollars for security fraud and other violations. Johnson and

Johnson have agreed to pay about 2.2 billion dollars as penalty and other fines for....corruption in kickbacks to doctors and pharmacies.

In 2013, more than 50 doctors, pharmacists and staff were arrested for illegal selling of drugs and controlled prescriptions in Michigan, USA. One of the pharmacists was jailed for more than 17 years.

"Everybody can be corrupted," 84 year old former crime boss, James "Whitney" Bulger said in a

James Whitney Bulger

documentary filmed in USA in 2013, "money is the common denominator," as reported by Sandy Cohen in the Associated Press.

All this happened due to the greed in America. While real estate values dropped by more than 50% in USA during 2007-2011, in India prices more than doubled during the same period.

Corruption in America is widespread

•

Chapter 7

Guns and Crimes

In August of 2013, ex-Deputy Prime Minister of Australia, Tim Fischer, in joining Pier Morgan Live on CNN said,

"80 people are killed by guns in the United States every single day. People who are thinking of going to the USA on business, vacation and trips, should think carefully about it given the statistical facts that you are 15 times more likely to be shot dead in the USA than in Australia, per capita per million people."

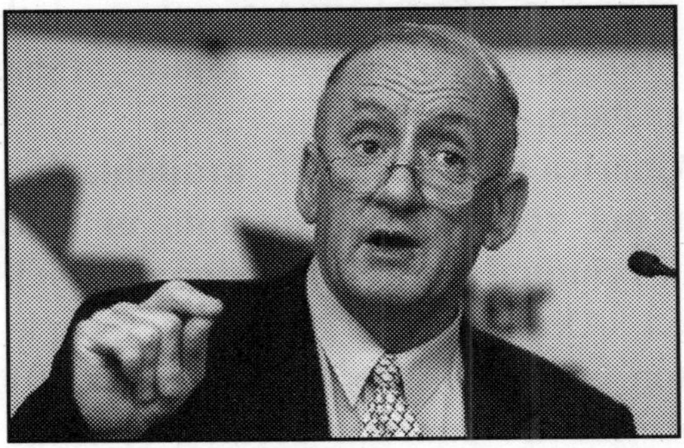

Ex-deputy Prime Minister of Australia - Tim Fischer

Mr. Fischer was speaking, after a 22 years old Australian student, Christopher Lane, was killed just five days earlier in Duncan, Oklahoma, USA by three teenagers. The motive, "there was nothing better to do, just for the fun of it," according to the Police Chief Ford. "We were going to kill somebody" the teenagers said.

Nearly two decades ago, Tim Fischer championed Australia's gun control reforms, an effort that has virtually eliminated firearm crimes in the country.

"Just for the record, Australia has had zero gun massacres since 1996." Fischer appealed to American authorities to follow in the footsteps his nation imprinted in the late 1990s, "We don't have gun shows where you can walk up and not even be subject to a background check is one of the most dumbest decisions so far in the litany of agony over the gun laws and gun policies of the NRA and the USA."

The purpose of a gun is to kill in a crime, defense or hunting. A crime is a wrong doing classified by the State or Congress and is an offense against a public law. A Jail is a facility where people are forced to live and lose their freedom which a normal citizen enjoys. Jails protect society from criminals, deter future offenders and rehabilitate them.

In America guns are easily available and some of them do not require any permits or background checks for criminal record or having mental illness.

Aaron Alexis, who killed 12 people at the Washington Navy Yard on September of 2013, had a history of violence and was accused of firing guns in anger, was arrested twice, and was also treated for serious mental problems. This did not prohibit him from legally purchasing the shot guns he used to kill those people and injuring many more. He simply went out of state, showed his driver's license and bought the guns, legally.

Mother of a six year old daughter, Emilie, said, "We brought Emilie home from the hospital on Mother's day, Alisa wrote in her blog 'theparkerfive.wordpress.com' Emilie was one of the 20 children massacred at Sandy Hook Elementary School in December 2012.

''And I always found it fitting they were celebrated at the same time. She was my first baby, and it was my first Mother's day.'' Robbie Parker spoke to the reporters before the memorial service, "She was beautiful, she was always smiling," he said. "I'm so blessed to be her dad.''

In America, nearly 100,000 people will be shot this year out of which about 17,000 will be children younger than 19, according to the Brady Campaign to Prevent Gun Violence. That volume speaks unflattering volumes about our seriousness. As does a politico report that support is softening for laws that would expand background checks and impose other common sense restrictions on gun ownership.

A Florida state legislature panel just voted to support a bill allowing teachers to bring guns to school. Once again, the nation endorses the Orwellian logic, which would "solve" the problem of too many guns, the Free Press said, **''Each head of a household in Nelson, Georgia, must own gun and ammunition to provide safety for city and residents."** Council members of Nelson voted unanimously to approve the Family Protection Ordinance, according to the Toronto Star;

Such mandatory gun ownership measures reflect a growing divide in the wake of the Newton massacre as PRESIDENT OBAMA champions more gun control, the powerful National Rifle Association gun lobby maintains that more guns keep people safe, according to the Star;

A campaign promising free shotguns for people to protect themselves has divided residents in the community still reeling from shooting that killed six people, left a congresswoman and several others wounded, and made Tucson a symbol of gun violence of America;

The Armed Citizen Project is part of a campaign to give shotguns to single women and homeowners in the neighborhoods of Tucson, Arizona. **"Criminals have no desire to die in your hallway. We want to use that fear,"** Kyle Coplen, the Founder of the Project said, according to a report published in Toronto Star;

People behind the project say that shotguns are easy to use and don't require precise aim when shooting, making them perfect home protection weapon. **"The goal is to arm hundreds of people in Tucson, Houston, Chicago, New York , Detroit and at least 10 other cities by the end of the year."**

Allan M. Gottlieb, founder of the Second Amendment Foundation, said that he expects to see more gun giveaways as US President Obama and other leaders call for gun restrictions, according to Toronto Star.

In many states of America, there are no restrictions and background checks to buy a short gun. However to own a conceal firearm, one needs a permit which has been surging since 2007. Florida has doubled the concealed-carry permits in five years. Some leaders in law enforcement call the increasing requests for conceal-carry permits unwelcome, citing safety concerns.

Craig Steckler
President of the International Association of Chief of Police

Craig Steckler, President of the International Association of Chief of Police, said he could remember only "one instance which some one defended himself" with a firearm during his 21 years as police chief in Fremont, CA. Otherwise, "It's a whole lot of cases of guns not being used in a way they are designed: kids shooting themselves, gun cleaning accidents, crime of passion, that sort of things," according to The Globe and Mail.

Crime

About three million Americans are in jails plus another five million are on parole, this is nearly 3% of the population of America. On top of these, there are many more criminals wondering around on the streets of America. All the big cities like New York, Los Angeles, Chicago, Miami, Dallas, Detroit have high degree of crime. Visitors are warned of certain areas of the cities.

There have been cases where people have been robbed or killed to snatch a purse, piece of jewelry etc.

"I just murdered my grandson," 74 years old grandmother, Sandra Layne of Michigan told the police in May of 2012, that she killed her grandson. She came on front door walking towards police officers with .40 caliber Glock handguns in her hand. The former school teacher, mother of 5 and grandmother of nine children killed her grandson with eight bullets. 17 years old, Jonathan Holfman, called 911 and pleaded for help, then was shot by the grandmother. Police said that Jonathan was shot during the call.

Michael Vanderlinden

Dad strangled his 4 and 7 years old sons and then stabbed his wife before dying in a car crash. Police said that Michael Vanderlinden used "81/2" butcher knife to kill them. Police said that Michael, 38, had alcohol and drug problems and was to move out of the house due to family problem. He pleaded to his wife not to leave him again, after he had argument with her and grabbed her neck and police was called.

Patrick Mikes Jr. 21 was charged for killing his dad. **His younger brother, Andrew, testified that his brother and father had a tense relationship. Earlier, his father cancelled a credit card which Patrick had used for $100 to $200 for out of town trip.** Police said that father died of at least 4 blows to head, possibly from a silver metal baseball found in the basement.

Peterson, an ex-policeman of Chicago, was called an untouchable, unflappable and a killer. "I am sick of being called sinister" said accused wife murderer Drew Peterson, who has been imprisoned for the past 3 years waiting for the trial for the death of his third wife, Kathleen Savio, and is the chief suspect of his fourth wife, Stacey Peterson. In May 2012, Peterson was found guilty of killing his third wife Kathleen Savoi. In March of 2004, Savio was found drowned in bath tub of her house and her death was declared as accidental. Three years later, his 23 year old wife disappeared.

Keep Assault Weapons off U.S. streets, that is the voice of many Americans after the shooting in Aurora, Colorado where 70 people were shot with an assault weapon AK47 at Movie Theater showing a Batman film 'The Dark Knight Rises" out of which 12 people died. **President Obama told the members of National Urban League at their annual convention in New Orleans in July of 2012. "AK47 belong to in the hands of soldiers not in the hands of criminals, that they belong to the**

battlefield of war, not to the streets of our cities." In USA, most of the guns are available and could be bought on the counters of stores with 24 hours waiting period.

There have been many mass shooting in Schools and other places in America in 2012 alone. In Newton, Connecticut school shooting, at least seven students died along with many others in December.

Wisconsin
Sikh temple gunman

In August of 2012, in a mass shooting in Sikh temple, six people were shot dead when a gun man entered the temple and mercilessly shot innocent devotees including the priests. The shooter did not know anybody in the temple. Later, shooter killed himself.

Jared Lee Loughner
Tucson Arizona shooter

In April of 2012 people were killed and three wounded in Christian College shooting in Oakland. Again the shooter had the most dangerous guns which are easily available in the stores.

In January of 2012, a gunman opened a shooting outside a grocery store in Tuscan, Arizona killing 6 people including a 9 years old student. At least 12 other got wounded. A congress woman, Gabrielle Giffords, was severely wounded.

National Rifle Association (NRA) is the strongest defendant of gun ownership in USA. In the recent school shooting, **NRA officials stated that all the schools should have security people at the campus to protect the children.** After the shooting in a movie theater where 12 people died and more than 50 wounded, NRA officials claimed that if the people had guns, there would have been fewer killings. Basically the NRA is promoting to have guns all the time in your possession so that if other person start shooting, you can shot back to stop the violence.

Wayne LaPierre

Even President Obama had tears in his eyes
for the victims during the news conference

A protest in Washington, D.C. on December 17.
The U.S. has 300 million people and 310 million registered guns.

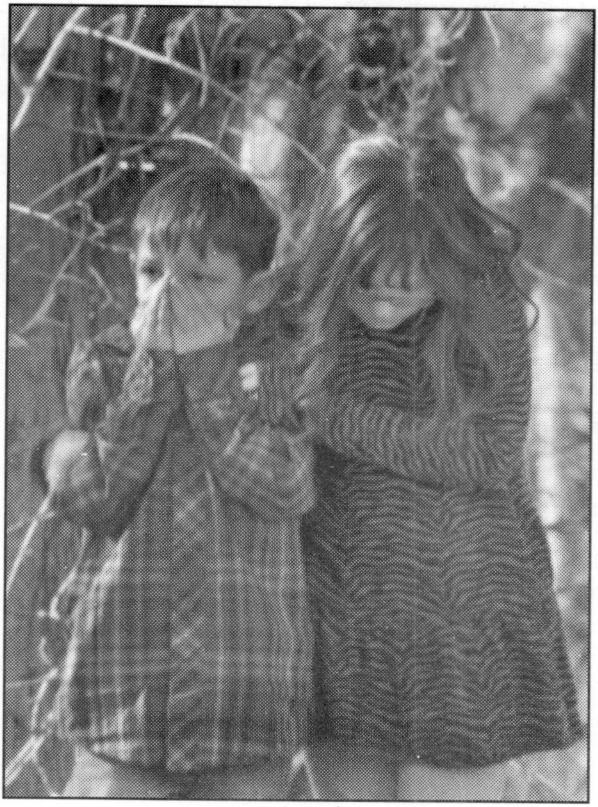

Children wait outside
Sandy Hook Elementary School
in Newtown, Connecticut,
on December 14,
after the shootout.

In India, there are about 320,000 people in jails for a population of about 1,200 million compared to 3,000,000 Americans in the jails for a population of about 320 million. Number of people in jails, are 40 times per capita in America than that in India.

In America, there are more guns than the population, but in India, the guns are not available in the open. About 3% of the population owns guns in India and deaths by the guns per capita are less than 1/10th of that of America.

In September of 2013, Howard Schultz, CEO of Starbucks requested its customers not to bring guns at his stores. He made a request only to the customers, but not a ban. Few weeks earlier, one of his stores was robbed in Florida. Mr. Schultz justified the request by saying that his stores are for relaxation of the customers where they can feel safe.

People are safer from gun crimes in India than Americans are in their country. So Indians have better culture than the Americans.

Safe and peaceful living is a better culture.

Chapter 8

Drugs, Drinking and Gambling

"Men crave alcohol when they're shown images of booze, but women covet it when they see photos of a messy kitchen or a screaming infant." Gabrielle Glaser wrote in her book, "Her Best-Kept Secret: Why Women Drink-and How They Can Regain Control." "With women in their 40's and 50's, it is a response to stress or at a loss of a parent or during divorce or when their last child moved out to go away to school."

Drinking is at all time high in America. I believe that "the richer the country, the worst is the problem." The alcohol is cheaper and easily available, especially in America where one can buy alcohol almost at any time at a corner store. According to CDC (Center for Disease Control and Prevention), **42% of men and 22% of women, drink in America.** Economic cost of excessive drinking is more than $220 billion.

There are bars all over the cities which are open till late night. As some of the addicted people run short of money, they turn into stealing, robbing and even seriously hurting people. Many people run into trouble with law over speeding, car accidents due to alcohol and lose their licenses. There is big problem of drinking at work places. Recently, there have been the incidences where factory workers have lost their jobs due to drinking at lunch hours.

On the average, 10,000-12,000 people die in America due to DUI (Drinking Under Influence) related accidents and about one million arrested each year. 90% of all drunk driving happens after drinking with family, friends and co-workers.

"I never worried about being driven to drink, I only worry about being driven home," W.C.Field wrote in a blog.

"Since Sept 11 terror attack, over 130,000 men, women and children have died in USA as a result of drunk driving. Laws providing a deterrent are not enough; we need to address the behavior in

our culture that put drunk drivers on the road. It is time to stand up, admit that as a culture, we drink together and let each other drive away," another person, Allen D.Porter wrote.

Drugs

Drugs are another household problem. **It is said that United States is the largest user of drugs.** Drugs come from all over the world through Mexico and other countries by road, sea or by air. Even in the schools, drugs are available. Hollywood is one of the most popular places for drug users. Many stars and their children are known to be addicted. Some of them have been sent to jail for the possession of drugs.

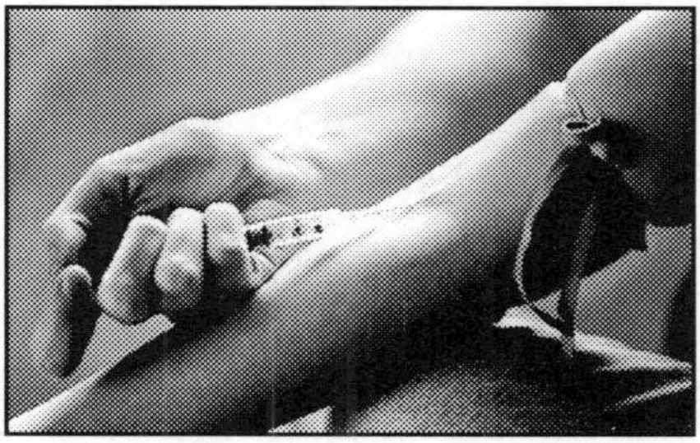

Michael Douglas

Michael Douglas and Catherine Zeta-Jones only just got through the nightmare of Michael's throat cancer (he's in remission) and now they fear for their lives again with potential death threats from a Mexican drug cartel.

When you think of Hollywood, there are three things that come to mind, fame, sex, and drugs. It seems like anyone who is attracted to the fame aspect of Hollywood, manages to get caught up in one of the later two. Maybe it's less prevalent, than it appears, but too often we hear of celebrity deaths due to drug use. Probably the most recent was Corey Haim's death due to an accident overdose. But why does it affect those in Hollywood? What is it about the lifestyle that causes such a large group of people to struggle? Some say it's the fame, the stress, and others will say it is just as rampant in the regular society and Hollywood is no different. Since none of my friends use, I'm pretty sure it's not as prevalent everywhere else as it is in Hollywood.

Redmond James Fawcett O'Neal, born January 30, 1985, in Los Angeles. In April 2009, on probation for driving under the influence, Redmond was arrested for possession of narcotics

Michael Jackson

Michael Jackson was an American recording artist and businessman. Often referred to as the "King of Pop", is recognized as the most successful entertainer of all time by Guinness World Records.

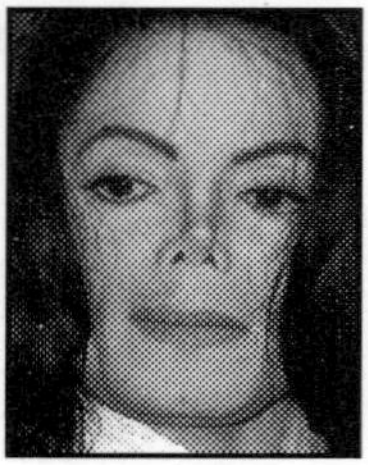

Aspects of Jackson's personal life, including his changing appearance, personal relationships, and behavior, generated controversy. In the mid 1990s, he was accused of child sexual abuse, but the cases were settled out of court for millions of dollars and no formal charges were brought. In 2005, he was tried and acquitted of further child sexual abuse allegations and several other charges after the jury found him not guilty on all counts.

While preparing for his concert series titled, "This is It", Jackson died of acute propofol and benzodiazepine intoxication on June 25, 2009, after suffering from cardiac arrest.

Elvis Presley

Elvis Presley died in 1977—best known for his singing and swaying hips. He also acted in several movies like ''Love me Tender.'' Although there is a long standing belief that he is not truly dead due to the hero worship many gave him. Prescription drug abuse severely deteriorated his health, and he died suddenly in 1977 at the age of 42. His death report states, cardiac arrhythmia.

Marilyn Monroe

Marilyn Monroe was an American actress, model, and singer, who became a major sex symbol, starring in a number of commercially successful motion pictures during the 1950s and early 1960s.

The final years of Monroe's life were marked by illness, personal problems, and a reputation for unreliability and being difficult to work with. **The circumstances of her death, from an overdose of barbiturates, have been the discussion for a long time.** Though officially classified as a "probable suicide" the possibility of an accidental overdose, have not been ruled out.

Whitney Houston

Whitney Elizabeth Houston was an American recording artist, actress and model. In 2009, the Guinness World records cited her as the most awarded female actress of all time.

On February 11, 2012, Houston was found dead in her guest room at the Beverly Hilton Hotel, in Beverly Hills, California. Toxicology reports showed that **she had accidentally drowned in the bathtub due to the effects of chronic cocaine use and heart disease.**

There is a long list of many famous people who were convicted, arrested or died due to drugs or drunk driving.

Princess Diana

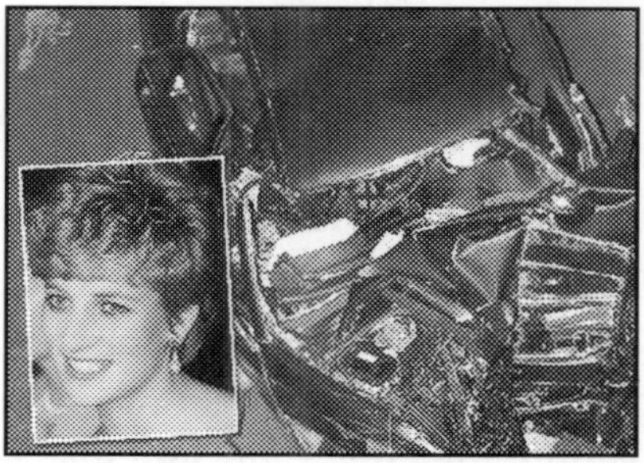

After her divorce with Prince Charles, she was romantically involved with Dodi-Al-Fyed with whom she was traveling with in Paris on August 30, 1997 and died in car accident. **The toxicology report showed that the driver was intoxicated.**

Paris Hilton

She was arrested in September of 2006, and was sent to 3 years probation. Later she was arrested again and sent to jail for 45 days.

Lindsay Lohan

She was arrested in the year of 2007 for DUI.

Mel Gibson

In 2006 Mel Gibson ended up with probation for DUI. He was further subjected to a 90 day alcohol-abuse program, 12 months of Alcohol Anonymous meetings and was fined with a license suspension.

Tim Allen

Tim Allen, was caught for drug smuggling in 1978 at Kalamazoo/Battle Creek Airport for carrying cocaine. In exchange for not having to go to prison for life, as was the maximum penalty that could have been leveled against him, Allen plead guilty and subsequently ratted out the other drug dealers he knew. This got his potential sentence reduced from life imprisonment. He ended up serving about 2 years in a Federal Correctional Institution. Further he was charged with DUI in 1997.

Glen Campbell

In November of 2003, Glen crashed his BMW into another car and was arrested for DUI and sent to jail for 10 days.

Mike Tyson

In 2006 was arrested for DUI and possession of cocaine.

Gambling

Las Vegas, Nevada, is home to about 80 casinos. Nevada was the first state in the US to legalize gambling. By the 1960s, Las Vegas had more than 20 casinos and was the most popular destination in the USA and in the world.

The Nevada Legislature was motivated to build on the tourism boom after the completion of Hoover Dam. The move for making gambling legal also grew out of concerns that the flourishing illegal gambling was corrupting law enforcement and prohibition was unenforceable.

Hollywood stars invested in the city and came to play there. The top entertainers from around the globe have been seen on stages across the city. Today the city hosts hundreds of resorts and other entertainment facilities but the focus then and now has always been on the luxurious gaming operations.

One more gambling Mecca can be found in Atlantic City, New Jersey, long known as a vacation spot due to

its position on the Atlantic shore. There are about 15 casinos in Atlantic City.

Average casino employs 7,000 to 10,000 people. Large casinos employ more than 20,000 persons. Most of the population of about 2 million people in Metro Las Vegas, work in casinos or related industries. For many years, Las Vegas was the fastest growing city in the United States. The property values were rising very fast and the unemployment was one of the lowest in the country. Due to downturn in the economy, there have been steady layoffs since 2007 and the property values dropped by more than half. Also the unemployment rose, to be one of the highest in the country. Recently, the economy and the real estate values are recovering.

The casinos count their winning from small players. Even though there are special VIP rooms and entertainment for high rollers, but they still make most of the money from the smaller players. It is said that average player loses $70-$80 a day. Many casinos expect 15,000-20,000 customers every day.

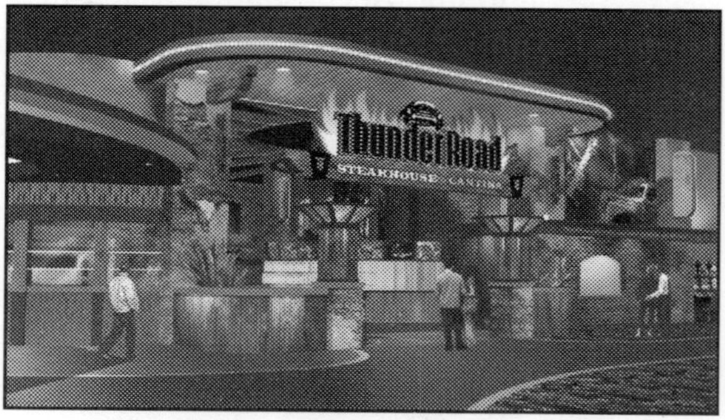

A large number of the players are senior citizens who use these places as part of their entertainment centers. To attract customers, casinos give them free food, hotel rooms, gifts, entertainment shows and

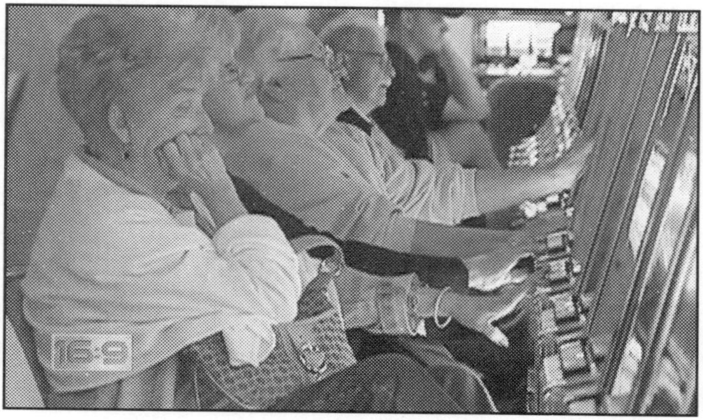

sometimes even the airline tickets, depending upon the money and time the customers play in the casinos. Casinos rate the players like 7 stars, platinum, diamond, gold or many other ways and issue a player's card just like a credit card. Every time players play, they insert those cards in the slot machine or give it to the dealers to obtain bonus points for free-bees. More you play, higher the rating you get. Higher rating means, you have spent more money and time on gambling. More money you spend more loses at the casinos, which usually happens.

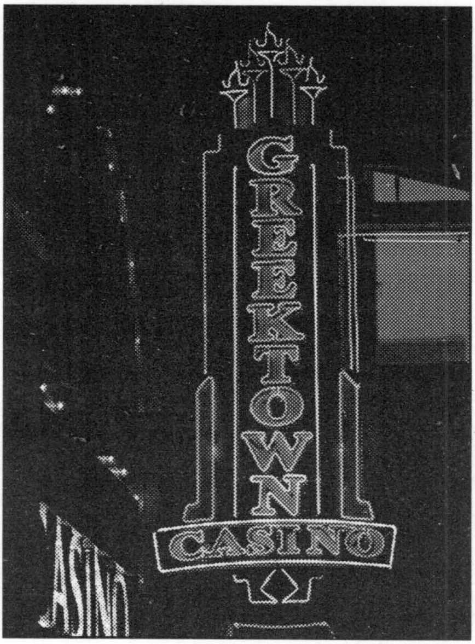

Many people are known to have lost their homes, businesses and marriages due to gambling in casinos. In earlier days, people would go to Las Vegas for 3-4 days, took some money, lose/win on gambling, go for dinners, attend some shows and come home. To go to Las Vegas, usually takes 2-4 hours flight from most cities of America. Many people made it a habit to go there every 2-3 years.

Now casinos being next door, many of them got addicted with it. I heard a story about a person who sold his business for more than a million dollars,

moved to a city where the casino was, lost all his money, got divorced and eventually did suicide. Another couple, who owned many properties, operated restaurant for many years, gambled whole night after closing of their business. They lost all the properties, business, their own house and got divorced. Now they are renting separately and working for other people.

Most casinos have regular patrons. There are various types of games. One group is called the table games which include Black Jacks, Craps and Roulette etc. Others are called slot machines. Normally the slot machine section is much larger than the table section. There are so many different types of slot machines now days. Older days, the players had to put coins each time they push the handle, it was running at the slow speed. Now, when you put money in these machines, the machine gives you a credit for that amount of money. You just select the amount you want to play by pressing a button, and bet is played. It is a much faster way to gamble and also a faster way to lose money without manual labor of pushing the handle every time. When you finish with one machine, it gives you a credit slip which you can easily reuse in that machine or in any other

machine in that casino. The casino saves lot of manual labor and the players lose money much faster. The casinos always keep on searching the ways to quickly empty the pockets of the customers.

At the table section, there are group of people playing together, while on the slot machines, only one player plays at a time. Larger casinos have more than 10,000 slot machines. Usually the players sitting at the slot machines are very serious as they keep putting money in those machines and expect them to roll out big money, which do happens once a while. Usually these people don't talk to anybody or even do not eat much food but drinking is very common. Some casinos offer free alcohol so, more a customer drinks, more he/she will tend to gamble.

These casinos have very attractive way to bring customers and keep them coming back. Some of the parking lot attendants at VIP section do remember the names of their regular customers. **Further the host, at the gaming tables addresses the customers by their names, signifying their importance. They also invite these customers for dinners on their birthdays and anniversaries and offer them free gifts on Christmas and other occasions. For many, it has become their way of life.**

There is no new creation of wealth in gambling, except that it changes hands from public to the casinos and brings tax to the governments. Many of the state

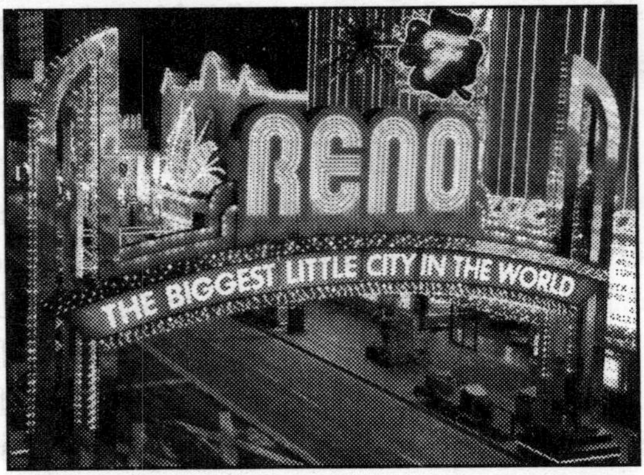

governments had been running in deficit and after watching Las Vegas, they also allowed gambling. Until 1978, only Nevada state had legal gambling, then the state of New Jersey allowed in Atlantic City, due to deficit in the state budget. State governments receive billions of dollars from casinos who in turn empty the pockets of the seniors and the poor.

Another major source of government revenue is from lottery tickets. A growing opposition by the public to tax increases was a leading factor in establishing state-run lotteries in the 20th century. New Hampshire was the first state to sponsor a lottery, followed by New York. The New Jersey lottery was successful because it stressed frequent action at low cost, and it returned a higher percentage of lottery revenues as prizes.

One of the most well known lotteries was the Irish sweepstakes which began about 80 years ago. Most people who buy the lottery tickets are the lower middle class to poor people. We have heard people spending as much as 50% of their pay checks to purchase the lottery tickets. When the draw becomes extra ordinary large, more people buy these tickets. The fact is, that in the bigger draws, the odds of winning is even smaller.

In India, women drinking are very low. There is a complete prohibition in certain states of India. Men's drinking is more common in North than in South. Moreover, alcohol is very expensive for a common man. Drinking is not socially accepted in India. There is hardly any casino in India and drugs may be popular among some very few rich families only.

India does not have casinos resulting in less financial losses and less divorces.

Indian culture is superior to the American culture.

●

Chapter 9

Divorce, Children and Suicide

Divorce is the termination of marital union, the cancelling of the legal duties and responsibilities of marriage.

The divorce rate in the United States is one of the highest in the world. More than 50% of the marriages end up in divorce. Children of divorce are about fifty percent in America. Women initiate more divorce than men and 60% of them live under poverty in America.

A decision to divorce is forced upon a child. Divorce traumatizes children. When one parent leaves, he

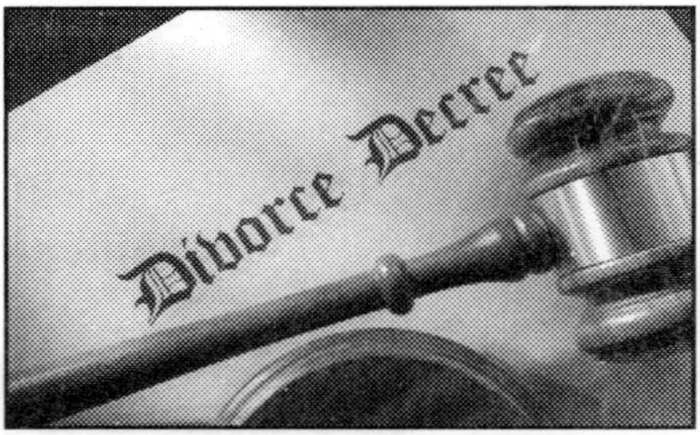

or she may fear the other one will follow. **Children worry about what is going to happen to them. They are often concerned with their own security,** not with their parent's happiness. Children may express anger and hostility and school performance may be impaired. Children may also get depressed.

In a blog, Kate, an American, wrote, "I think divorce has done a lot to tear down our family - 50% families end up in divorce. Coming from a divorced family, **I was constantly pulled by each parent like fighting in tug of war.** I had split time, split holidays, two different upbringings. I had to conform to the ideas and upbringing of two step parents;

All because of that one decision of them to have divorce, I was stripped of my innocence by a perverse stepfather. My father no longer will speak to me or

anything to do with me since I was sixteen and had belief of my own. And my mother is emotionally unstable and we don't have great relationship;

If I could have a family that is together and can depend on, but I had no control over it. It is the way it is. Then there are thousands of families like mine and it's all because of divorce and lack of being a true family;

Coming from an American point of view, I think that the fact is that we do not have family as part of our happiness is one of the saddest things about our culture in comparison to Indian."

There are many causes for divorce including no trust, financial difficulties, addictions, lack of communication, abuse etc. A common response to divorce is to seek vengeance.

Very few people going into a divorce for the first time can anticipate how a marital breakdown deranges their lives. In a divorce, income that once supported one household now supports two.

Gregory Peck

Gregory Peck was 5 years old when his parents got divorced in 1921. He was so devastated from it that years later in an interview with Cosmopolitan Magazine, he said "I don't care to talk about my childhood because it was so sad". According to his friends, the trauma he experienced at the time of his parent's divorce and the upheaval that followed triggered a long standing depression which never left him.

Glenn Beck

Glenn Beck, a very famous TV and Radio host, tried suicide in 1994. His mother drowned in a small boat which Glenn described as suicide. His step brother also committed suicide. At the age of 15, he got addicted to drugs.

Cory Monteith, a very famous movie and TV star suffered fatal drug overdose in July of 2013. Cory had spoken publicly about his history as a trouble teen that battled drugs and alcohol abuse. His parents divorced when he was 7 and started taking drugs at 13, went to 12 different schools before quitting at the age of 16. According to his friends, **he was very devastated from his parent's divorce.**

Cory Monteith

Money in a divorce always becomes a problem. Child support payments cause monetary strain on both parents, which directly affects the children. The marital home may be sold as part of the property settlement. In some instances, one of the parents may have to relocate. Children have to adjust to new schools.

Many friends are lost during divorce. Husband and wife may keep their individual friends; the friends the couple made together as a married couple often drift away. Sometimes, people don't want to take sides, but often people drift away because divorce can be very threatening, particularly when a couple senses problems in their own home.

Family beyond the parents can be disrupted by divorce. Step families become very complicated. Holidays and birthdays after a divorce can be very difficult. The first birthday, that first anything is difficult for children.

Some marriages should end. Domestic violence is the reason to end a marriage.

Suicide

Suicide is very common among seniors. A U.S. study says the rate for white men over 85 was 45 per 100,000 in 2007 and about 85 percent of elderly suicide was of men, with someone taking their life every 97 minutes, as per Postmedia News by David Sherman.

As per David, it often plays out like this. **"An elderly man is in pain, lonely, bored, impoverished, tired, hungry and depressed.** There is a good chance he is chronically ill - emphysema, prostate cancer, a heart condition, arthritis or any number of things. He might be in a one-room apartment, a senior's residence, or he is rambling around the house he lived in when the kids were at home and the wife was alive. But now, the spouse is dead and his children have moved on and almost every movement is a painful reminder of the years of joys;

Like most people of his age, he has shelves of pills - for pain, for sleeping, for anxiety, which is really a form of raging boredom. And probably the pills to fight the inevitable depression fueled by all of the above. **No one knows his ultimate decision to swallow a bottle of booze and a bottle or two of pills - a cocktail that will end it all;**

More likely his death will be chalked up to natural causes. He was old and sick and his number was up, it will be said. The death certificate will be signed and his suicide will go unrecognized. And the older you are, the higher the rate. The fact that many go unreported makes it difficult to get a fix on the exact numbers, some doctors' say" David wrote.

Paul Oliver

The suicide is very high in professional sports. Paul Oliver, a defensive back of University of Georgia killed himself with gunshot in 2013. He left behind his wife and two children.

Another famous player, Junior Seau, 43, Hall of Fame linebacker of San Diego Chargers shot himself.

Junior Seau

Another famous player, Jovan Belcher 25, killed himself after killing his girl friend in 2012. Mr. Belcher played for Kansas City Chief as inside linebacker.

Jovan Belcher

In the military, suicide rate has trippled since 2004 to almost one a day. "It drives me crazy," the Army Deputy Undersecretary Thomas Hawley said. They could not figure out the reason for such an increase in the rate of suicide.

Divorce rate in India is 1.1% compared to over 50% in America. Children's care is the top most priority for the Indian parents than their own. They sacrifice their own happiness for the children.

Indian culture is superior to the American culture.

Chapter 10

Rapes, Sports and Churches

I was reading a very famous book 'You can heal your life' written by an American author, Louise Hay. More than 40 million copies of this book have been sold, worldwide.

I found this book to be very useful in terms of teaching the public, the reasons of diseases and the natural way of healing them. **Ms. Hay has done a lot of good to the humanity, helping millions of people through seminars and through her books but, she was helpless in most of her early childhood life.** Ms. Hay was from a poor family. Her step father was a violent man.

Louise L Hay

At the age of 5, she was raped by a neighbor who was later sentenced for 15 years. She was sexually abused most of her early life and left school at the age of 15 when she got pregnant. Later, when she was diagnosed with cervical cancer, she blamed it to her sexual abuse through the years of her life and holding her resentment. She refused conventional way of treatment and began a process of forgiveness and nutrition and got rid of the cancer that way.

Justin Bieber, a famous singer Pop star, was brought up by a divorced and sexually abused mother, Pattie Mallette. She had an alcoholic and abusive father who left her when she was 2. **"When my father left, it ripped a hole in my heart. The wound of being abandoned travels deep and forever changes you,"** Ms. Mallette wrote in her book "Nowhere But Up." She was raised in Canada.

Justin Bieber with mother

Talking about her abused life, she further wrote, **"I was sexually violated so many times, as the years went by it began to feel normal,** it is strange marriage - in knowing something wrong yet at the same time finding it familiar and common place. I feel like, with my past, I didn't deserve to have the most amazing child that I have. **I did not tell him my story until he was about 12 years old, he heard for the first time and tears came in his eyes."**

She was sexually molested by a male baby sitter, grand father of one of her friend, neighbors. Sexual abuse continued until 14, followed by a date rape at 15. She started relationship with Jimmy Bieber at 15 and got pregnant with Justin.

Rapes have destroyed lives of thousands and thousands of people in America from early age to the elderly people. According to New York Times, per capita, rapes in New York are three times more than those in Mumbai, India.

According to Detroit Free Press, a 58 year old Farmington Hills substitute teacher was charged with having sexual contact on March 19, 2013, with a 13 year old raping during school hour.

In January, a 30 year old substitute musical teacher was sentenced to 5 years in prison for having sex with a 16 year-old student and exchanging nude cell phone photos and video with two girls. Also in January, a 38-year old middle school teacher in West Branch was charged with three counts of first-degree criminal sexual conduct, accused of engaging in oral sex with a male student who was between the age of 13 and 16.

Madona was raped at knife point on the top of a New York building when she was young, as per "Harper Bazaar." "First year I was held at a gun point, raped on the roof top of a building, I was dragged with a knife at my back and had my apartment broken into 3 times."

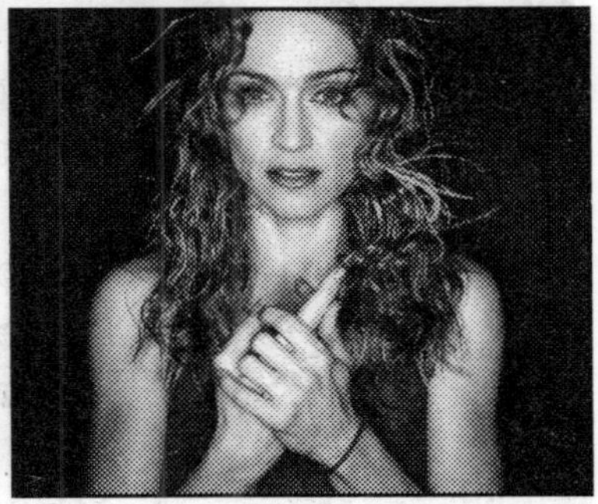

Madona

The researchers defined rape as completed forced penetration, forced penetration facilitated by drugs or alcohol, or attempted forced penetration. By that definition, it is estimated that 1.3 million American women may be the victims of rape or attempted rape every year.

Commenting on a 2010 survey by US government on rape and domestic violence—**"that almost one in five women has been raped in her life time is very striking and, I think, will be surprising to a lot of people,"** said Linda C. Degutis, director of the National Center for Injury Prevention and Control at the Centers for Disease Control and Prevention. "I don't think we've really known that it was this way prevalent in the population," she said. Sexual violence affects women disproportionately, the researcher found.

Military Sex Abuse

President Obama holding an emergency meeting with his top military officers and Defense Secretary

Chuck Hagel

Chuck Hagel, on the report of increased sex assault in the military, said "There is no silver bullet to solving this problem," Obama told reporters. "This is going to require a sustained effort." Earlier, the U.S. Department of Defense reported 26,000 men and women had been exposed to unwanted sexual contacts between 2011 and 2012, a 40% increase in such assaults over two years.

A former air force officer Russell William was convicted of sexually assaulting and murdering two women. **Officer Nichole Goddard reported that she was not the only person raped but there were six rapes in one week in her camp. Just a fraction of these cases were reported and even a smaller percentage was prosecuted,** reported Detroit Free Press. Soldiers who reported sexual assault say that, they experienced social and professional retaliation, a risk that some advocates say is enhanced because the military's current system requires victim to make such report to the commanders.

Russell William

Head of U S Air Force Anti-Sexual Assault Unit, Lt. Col. Jeffry Krusinski, (51), was arrested allegedly

Lt. Col. Jeffry Krusinski

grabbing a woman by the breast and buttocks in a parking lot not far from the Pentagon, reported by Reuters. An Arlington County Police spokesman said that Mr. Krusinski, was under influence of alcohol, and when he attempted to grab her a second time she was able to call the police who arrived in short time and detained him.

Churches

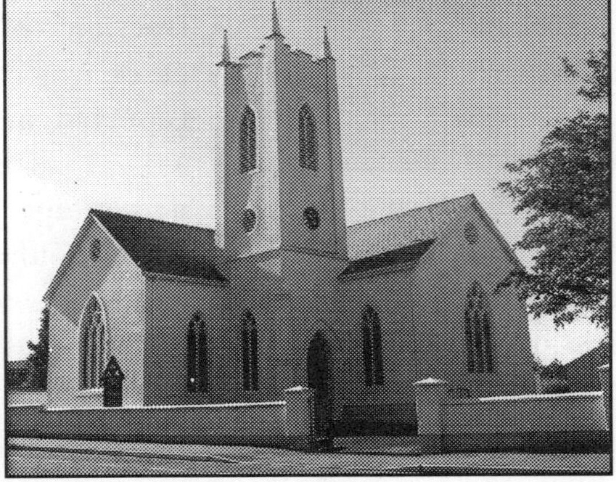

The rape of young children had been so common in Churches that hundreds of church officials, priests (some as old as 80 years old) have been convicted in court and many of them are in jails.

Few years earlier, the media started covering sexual abuse cases involving Catholic priests. Other victims began to come forward with their own allegations of abuse, resulting in more lawsuits and criminal cases. Since then, the problem of clerical abuse of minors has received significantly more attention from the law enforcement agencies. It is reported that more than 1000 civil cases have been filed and many settled by the churches for billions of dollars. Many Churches also closed or went bankrupt as they could not pay for the damages.

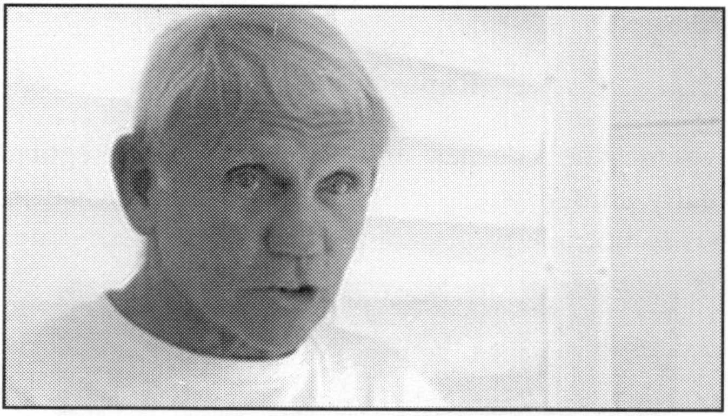

Richard John James Robinson, 73, was found guilty of 21 charges relating to offences against boys, all aged under 16, between 1959 and 1983. He was sentenced for 21 years.

Many Priests raped young boys as young as 10 years old who came to Church for some reason or the

other to help or for obtaining education, training etc. These young children when became older, started filing reports with the police. Earlier, when these young children complained to parents or school teachers, nobody would dare to go against the priests. Even the management, not only closed their eyes, but became a part of the problem. Hundreds and thousands of lives were destroyed and the crime kept on increasing.

A priest was jailed for 56 years for killing his fiancé's 24 years old daughter in USA to fulfill his desire to have sex with a dead body. According to police, Priest John White of Bloomfield Hills, Michigan confessed to killing Gay, in her home because he wanted to have sex with a dead body. White was engaged to Gay's mother and regularly looked after Gay's young son while she was working.

Rapes in Sports

In sports, the coaches and managers have regularly, sexually abused young children. The children had high hopes to become professional players and these coaches

Penn State University, Abington campus

lured them into giving false hopes to become famous players. The fact is that out of hundreds, if not thousands of players, one becomes a professional player earning millions of dollars, which is the American dream. This may be the reason that these abused children kept quiet. Further, when they complained, management and higher authorities closed their eyes to save the reputation and money coming to that institution.

Jerry Sandusky

One incident happened at Penn State University in Philadelphia. 68 years old, Jerry Sandusky, the assistant football coach of the most powerful college team of the United States, was found guilty on 45 counts of horrific child sex abuse and was sent to jail for life. A report prepared by the former **FBI Director, Louis Freeh said "The most powerful men at the Penn State failed to take steps for 14 years, to protect the children,**

FBI Director Louis Freeh

victimized by onetime assistant football coach, Jerry Sandusky." The report also said that a former head coach, Joe Paterno had an "integral part" in the decision to hide the facts tied to the sexual abuse of children.

Joe Paterno

Joe Paterno and other top Penn State officials hushed up child sex-abuse allegations against Jerry Sandusky for more than a decade for fear of bad publicity, allowing a former assistant coach to prey on young children.

The National Collegiate Athletic Association (NCAA) fined Penn State $60 million for failing to stop Sandusky, abusing children and stripped them of 112 football wins and cut down many scholarships. University removed the bronze statue of the coach Joe Paterno from the 107,000 seat football stadium. **Paterno failed to stop Sandusky even after one witness watched Sandusky sexually abusing young boy in men's shower, and reported to Paterno and higher authorities.** Now many executives, including the President of the University are on trial and probably will be in jail for long time.

A Police Officer was sentenced in Pennsylvania for 10 1/2 years in jail for travelling with 14 years old girl with intent to have illegal sex. The 60 years ex-police officer, married, travelled 900 miles to meet the girl and got arrested.

A raped police officer was offered cash to quit after being sidelined for nearly 3 years from her job. Denise Robindon, 38, says that she was raped and then effectively dismissed, because of it. She told the court that she was suspended and betrayed by Police Force. Since February of 2010, when she was raped and reported, she had not worked or received any paycheck. Instead of helping her, the police officer was sent to psychiatric assessment in the immediate aftermath of the assault. "After I reported this case, I was booted out of my residence. I was sent to Montreal and abandoned," officer said before sobbing. "I was suspended from my job; I lost my entire financial support, and now my career is ruined." The accuser was, finally, sent to jail.

Ex-Utica teacher who spent more than 30 years educating children got long prison for child pornography. Police found thousands of child pornographic images hidden in the basement of Gary Kliebert, 62. He was arrested in 2011 after police found thousands of videos and images of child pornography hidden in a concealed basement compartment. Further, Kliebert admitted to illegal sexual contact with an underage relative- which was confirmed through interviews with that person, authorities said.

He taught 4-6 grades, Christian Kpodjie, 53, was charged with 16 counts of sexual assault, 12 counts of sexual exploitation and 14 counts of assault.

Kearsley Peters, 56, a junior public school teacher, was charged with sexual assault on 2 twelve years old boys who were assaulted at the same house.

Alexis Wright, 30, pleaded guilty to multi counts of prostitution charges. She used her Fitness Studio as front for prostitution and made thousands in less than two years. She used a hidden camera to record sex acts with her client's without their knowledge.

Dr. Justin Onzuka was jailed for making pornographic movie and assaulting of 2 women while they were unconscious. 5 years earlier his license was suspended when it was found that he was a sex addict and had used pharmaceutical drugs. Dr. Onzuka admitted to the police that he had inappropriately touched his patients who were under anesthesia.

Dale Malesh, 62, a retired police officer was charged with having sexual relation with a 16 years old high school girl. Mr. Malesh was hired by the school as resource officer after his retirement. The officer faced a long jail term for third degree criminal sexual conduct.

A 22 years old woman was raped near Brooklyn College. He dragged the women down the alley, where he raped her and robbed of her cell phone. The entire incident was captured on video.

New York Times reported that per capita, New York had 3 times more rapes than Mumbai had in 2012.

A 20 year old tourist was raped after getting out of her cab near Madison Av in New York. The victim just came out of a night club and was returning to her hotel when a man grabbed her and dragged her into an alleyway and raped her.

As per UN Rape Statistics:
Reported rape cases per 100,000 (2010):

Canada	**1.7**
India	**1.8**
U.K.	**27.3**
USA	**28.1**
Australia	**28.6**

All rapes are not reported in every country. In USA it is estimated that only 16% rapes are reported. Rapes in America are 15 times more than those in India (2010) as per UN reports.

Indian culture is superior to the American culture.

Chapter 11

Narendra Modi and Vibrant Gujarat

During last two trips to India, I visited a place for orphans known as **Jeevan Prabhat in Gandhidham, Gujarat. This place with about 200 children aged from 6 months to 21 years old, built on 4 acres of land can be rated equal to 4-5 star hotels in USA. This was a spotless place.** The kitchen was equipped with most modern appliances. Fresh food was served to the children every day. The computer room has more than 15 newer and latest computers for the children.

The park and play ground is built on 2 acres of land and is beautifully landscaped and probably better than 90% of the parks in USA.

Everything in this place is first class and children are being brought up like in an upper middle class family atmosphere.

During my first trip in January of 2012, I stayed for 2 days in Gujarat which at the end I thought was not enough. So in January of 2013, I went there again for longer period of time. During this time I visited Gujarat's largest cities, Ahmadabad, Surat and the capital, Gandhinagar also.

Ahmedabad

Ahmedabad is the largest city of Gujarat state with a population of about 6 million people. In 2012, **Times of**

India named it the best city to live in India. Sabramati river flows through the city and all the beautiful parks are built on the side of this river.

Famous Kite Flying festival is celebrated on January 14-15 in this park every year. I happened to be there in 2013 and was surprised to see the magnitude of this function. There were at least 200 food and other stalls. A most modern stage with thousands of lights was set and sitting arrangements with beautiful chairs and sofas for more than 20,000 people in the park. Next day, the Chief Minister Modi addressed the large audience and celebrated the festival.

Heavy and Chemical industry, Textiles and Garments are the major industries of Ahmedabad.

Mahatma Gandhi was born in Gujarat and speeded up his national activities from Sabarmati Ashram located in Ahmedabad. Salt Satyagrah started from his Ashram here to Dandi. In 1942, Gandhi started his Quit India movement from Ahmedabad.

I visited the **Sabarmati Ashram** and sat in the room where Gandhi ji used to receive the guests. It was amazing feeling. The kitchen was very simple; one wonders how the dozens of people were served from there. The bedroom was very small. Such a great personality got freedom for India from such a small place, it's a magic. From this place I learned the will power of a single man. This gave me a big boost to move faster to clean India within 10-12 years the campaign of which we have already started a year ago. Clean India will encourage tourism. I believe, a clean India can generate up to $200 billion a year from tourism, as compared to the current amount of about $20 billion.

I read the big board at the Ashram and noticed the activities of Gandhiji, such as in the year:

1893—Went to S. Africa
1907—Satyagraha against discrimination and jailed in S. Africa
1920—Started non co-operation movement
1930—"Dandi March" protest
1942—Quit India movement
1947—Independence on 15th of August.

There were many more activities of Gandhi ji. He did more than 40 years of struggle to get a big nation free. This is a historical place of great significance. **This is India at the Sabarmati Ashram, a salute to Gandhiji.**

Gandhinagar

Gandhinagar, the capital of Gujarat, just 20 kilometer from Ahmedabad, was built in honor of Mahatma

Gandhi. I noticed the new roads, highways, new multi storeyed office buildings being built all over. The high cranes were visible from far distances. I was impressed with the development of the area.

I attended the world famous **"Vibrant Gujarat 2013"** a large industrial exhibition where exhibitors came from all over the world. The industries from plastic, paper, textile, electronics, high tech, auto and many others were there. There were big stalls from various

universities and other educational institutions. Thousands of visitors were all over the exhibition ground. **The display of the convertible car, made in Gujarat, was very impressive to me.**

Surat

Surat is the second most populous city of Gujarat with about 5 million people. The CCTV Camera installed by

the Commissioner, **Rakesh Asthana (IPS),** and helped by **Sudhir Sinha (IPS),** the former Commissioner of Police, which has contributed in the reduction of traffic violations and crimes in the city. **S R Rao (IAS),** former commissioner of Surat Municipal Corporation, has done miracles and made dirty Surat into the cleanest city with his team and public participation. Former Dy. Commissioner of SMC, **Ashwin Mehta,** described it well as he was also in the team.

Geeta Shroff, a dedicated social worker, helped thousands of people in educating and improving their lives. **Hamukh Patel (IPS),** DIG Surat Rural Police, as a good human being, works for "Parenting for Peace." These leading intellectual persons of the city prevent violence from the society. **All this is done under the guidance of the CM Narendra Modi's Long Vision.**

Surat is also known as the **Diamond City,** where world's 90% of rough diamonds are cut and polished. During my trip, I had the opportunity to visit a diamond factory, **SRK (Shree Ram Krishna Exports),** a multi

storey most modern building, equipped with latest technology and work force of over 5,000 people. This factory was finished with marble and granite flooring, elevators and was cleaner than many malls in USA.

What surprised me that every day, all 5000 employees are served freshly cooked lunch in different sittings, at the premises. I had the honor of having lunch along with CEO, **Mr. Govind Dholakia** and his staff at the same hall along with other workers. I was impressed with freshness of the food and efficiency with which they fed 5,000 people in less than 2 hours. I went to see another modern clothing factory, **Laxmipati Sarees** and met the CEO, **Mr. Sanjay Sarawagi,** a young man who has opened hundreds of stores. I was impressed with his management skills and vision.

Looking at all these CEOs and their developments, I wonder, if it will take 10 or 15 years, before India and in particular Gujarat, will be one of the most developed places of the world.

After all, it is the vision and hard work of the people of a country and the opportunities given by the government, which make that country stand above all others. One thing is already proven that Indians are one of the most intelligent people in the world.

All this was not possible without a strong leadership and vision of a leader and that is what exactly the Great State of Gujarat has, the Chief Minister, Narendra Modi.

Mr. Modi was born on September 17, 1950, 3rd of six children. He was confronted with many obstacles but overcame with courage. He struggled in the college and

university also. He always had been a fighter and a soldier. He did his post graduation in political science.

While teenager, Mr. Modi ran a tea stall, along with his brother, near the Bus Terminal. He entered politics at an early age. He was given charge of Association's student wing while he was completing Master's degree in political science.

In 1987, he joined the BJP (Bhartiya Janta Party) and entered politics full time. He became the General Secretary of BJP and was transferred to New Delhi in 1995. In 1996, he was promoted as the National Secretary of the party.

In 2001, he was appointed as the Chief Minister of Gujarat state, being the leader of BJP, having majority in the state assembly. In 2002's state assembly elections, his party won the majority and subsequently he won the elections in 2007 and in 2012. This is his 4th term as Chief Minister of Gujarat, a record in the state and probably in India.

Mr. Modi believes in small government and in privatization. He has only 20 ministers in his cabinet for such a large state, a record in India. He is a bachelor and known for his vision, honesty, dedication and hard work.

As I travelled the major cities of Gujarat, I found the fast lane highways all over the state. New constructions of roads, large complexes of industrial and commercial areas are being developed all over the state. 92% of roads are paved in Gujarat. **World Bank said that Gujarat**

offers an example of international best practice in road management.

The parks and river fronts have given a new meaning to people's lives. I have seen hundreds, if not thousands of people enjoying the water front which has been developed with beautiful gardens and fountains. During conversation, I found people were very happy and optimistic about their and the children's future in Gujarat.

I went to see the Kandla Port, which is one of the largest and busiest ports in India. I noticed new, huge

cranes under construction and many ships being loaded and unloaded while others were still waiting in the water for their turn.

Gujarat has achieved 100% enrolment in schools, in every locality for every child. In the last 10 years, the dropout rate in high school has dropped from 20% to 2% in 2011 (which is more than 20% in the USA). New colleges were increased from 442 to 1762 and universities increased from 11 to 42 during this period.

All this became possible since Mr. Modi became the leader of the State.

The Power in Gujarat was in very bad shape. In 2001, it ran a deficit of Rs.2250 cr. (about $4 billions) and 10 years later it was in surplus. Interest cost was 1225 cr. ($250 million) at 18%, Mr. Modi renegotiated, a savings of 500 cr. ($100million)

Distribution loss was 35%, cut down to 20%. Energy suppliers had manipulated the cost, renegotiated, a savings of 675 cr. ($130 million). Formed a power generating company, a transmission company and four distribution companies resulting in profit of Rs 533 cr. ($105 million) in 2011, just in 10 years. All the villages of Gujarat have the electricity. It has increased its installed generating capacity from 9600 MW to 15,700 MW. Considering peak demand of 11,200 MW, **Gujarat is a power surplus state.** It has 2500 MW of Wind Power and 600 MW of Solar Power.

In Gujarat, 550,000 water management structures have been built in the last 10 years. Micro irrigation is being aggressively pursued in over 800,000 acres.

In the urban transport, **Bus Rapid Transport System (BRTS)** has increased the bus efficiency and comfort of people. **BRTS has won the ITDP (USA)** award for showing, how large cities can reduce carbon emission with Smart System.

In IT field, **Gujarat's state wide network (GSWAN)** is the largest optical fiber network in Asia connecting all the government offices at all level including all 18,000 villages of Gujarat ensuring that public service can be delivered right at the door step of the common man in the village.

The government has made extensive use of IT for effective governance. The most outstanding and having substantial impact there is SWAGAT, which

started at state level in 2003. This has been extended to district and village level now. **It has won UN Public Service Award in 2010 and number of National Awards.**

Gujarat has launched 108 Free Emergency Services Centers to service all areas of Gujarat. The average response time is 18 minutes.

Twenty years ago, Gujarat's per capita income was much behind the neighboring, most industrial state of Maharashtra. According to RBI report of 2008, Gujarat's per capita income is at par now.

Wall Street Journal, in 2011 stated that 2 years earlier, investors pledged larger amount - upside of $450 Billion in the state of Gujarat. "Under Mr. Modi, Gujarat has acquired for aggressive wooing both domestic and foreign investments. **In 2008, Tata Group's Nano Car project, after political unrest, forced the company to flee the state of West Bengal to Gujarat. Ratan Tata,** the chief of Tata Group, said that under the leadership of Mr. Modi, Gujarat is not only seeing the industrial growth but also witnessing the rural development. **Mr. Tata praised Mr. Modi for his leadership and his ability to establish new ground for new industry.** India's two largest oil refineries and one of the world's largest automated coal terminals are located in Gujarat. General Motors, Mitsubishi Heavy Industries and Canada's Bombardier are located in Gujarat. Mr. Modi has the reputation of not only being honest but the man with inspiring leadership, integrity and good governance;

Mr. Modi has streamlined and nationalized procedures for land allocation and environmental clearance. For instance, the Tata Nano project took just three days to get the clearance. Mr. Modi has set the tone, minimum government and maximum governance."

In 2011, **G.V.L. Narasimha Rao** said "Nationwide there is a buzz that Narendra Modi's Gujarat has achieved a lot of progress and had made strides in development and progress largely on account of Mr. Modi's inspiring leadership, unquestioned integrity and good governance."

Amitabh Bachchan, a very famous actor, said "I am very impressed with Gujarat's development and felt like coming to the state again and again."

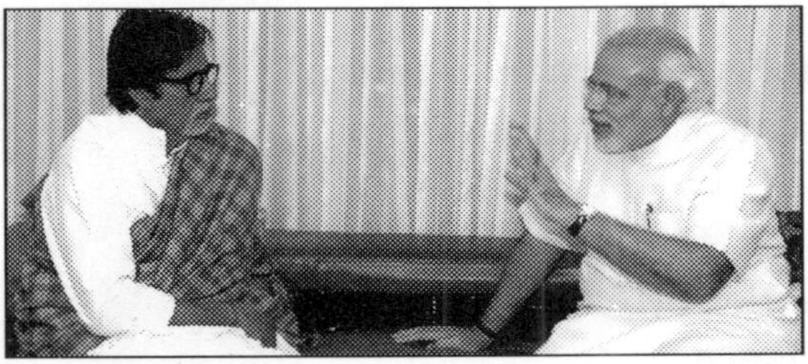

Akshay Kumar, another famous actor, who was awarded an Honorary Doctorate degree by a university in Canada, said "we were coming to this venue in the car and discussing the progress of this place in Gujarat, we saw committed lanes for buses and Wi Fi bus stops. This was amazing."

Anand Mahindra, CEO of Mahindra Group, one of the top 10 largest groups of India, said to Mr. Modi **"tell your critics you are doing a great job, the state administration is focused on outcome and not only in the show. You cannot afford not to be here."**

One of India's largest banks, ICICI's CEO, Chanda Kochhar stated "Gujarat is seen as the country's growth engine. Today when the world looks at India to drive world's growth, India looks at Gujarat to drive India's growth."

Mukesh Ambani, the richest man of India and CEO of the Reliance Group said **"the credit goes to the visionary, effective and passionate leadership provided by Mr. Modi. I have seen him run Gujarat more efficiently than I run the Reliance."**

A great follower of Mahatma Gandhi, Mr. Modi wrote in his book, "our action flows from Mahatma Gandhi's concept of trusteeship - that wealth belongs to the community and must be used for the welfare of the community."

At the inaugural VGSS session Mr. Modi said "today is the birthday of Swami Vivekanand, one of the greatest visionaries the world has ever produced. He envisioned a world driven by spiritual humanism that will enable everyone to have freedom, knowledge and happiness."

Mr. Modi has improved the lifestyle of the people of Gujarat and the country which is the part of Culture.

●

Chapter 12

Indians are richer than Americans

India was the richest country in the world till 18th century. Indian currency was at par with dollar in 1947, and one rupee was equal to 13 dollars in early 20th century. Early Indian inventions gave birth to many of today's technology.

Albert Einstein said "we owe a lot to the Indians, who taught us how to count, without which no worthwhile scientific discovery could have been made."

Mark Twain said "India is the cradle of the human race, the birth-place of human speech, the mother of history, the grandmother of legend, and the great grandmother of tradition. Our most valuable and most constructive materials in the history of man are treasured up in India only."

French scholar Romain Rolland said "If there is one place on the face of the earth where all the dreams of living men have found a home from the very earliest days when man began the dream of existence, it is India."

The world's first university was established in Takshila in 700BC. More than 10,000 students from all over the world studied over 60 subjects. The University of Nalanda built in the 4th century BC was one of the

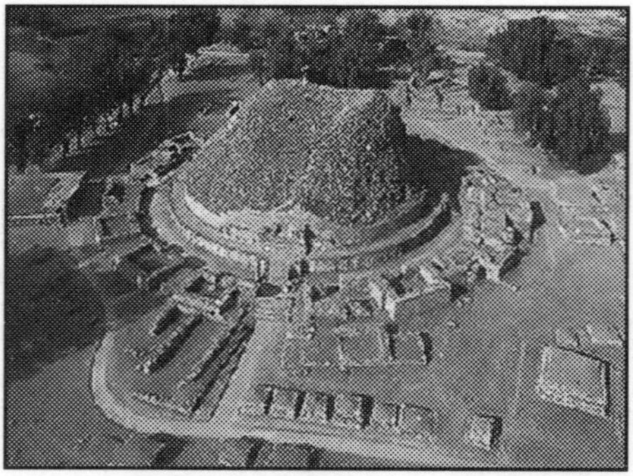

Takshshila University

greatest achievements of ancient India in the field of education.

The decimal system was developed in India. India invented the Number System. Zero was invented by Aryabhatta. Chess was invented in India.

A large number of doctors in America are Indians. Microsoft, IBM, Intel, NASA and many large American Corporations have employed thousands of Indians in the high posts. Recently Satya Nadella, an Indian born, was appointed as the CEO of Microsoft, one of the largest companies in America.

Average Indian is richer than Average American

United States economy is mostly based on the credit. It starts with the 12 Federal Reserve Banks who jointly are responsible for implementing the monetary policy set by the Federal Open Market Committee.

Federal Reserve Bank

The twelve regional Federal Reserve Banks were established as the operating arms of the nation's central banking system. Its primary functions are to promote favorable monetary policy, serve as a primary source of supervision and regulation.

The banks are allowed to lend 9-10 times the amount of deposits it receives from the customers, equities and other assets. The banks make money on the interest rate difference of what it pays to the depositors and what it receives from the borrowers. If the bank loses 10% of the amount, the entire equity of the bank could be lost. Because of it, many large financial institutions including, Lehman's Brothers, the fourth largest financial institution in the United States, failed during years 2007-2010.

For many years, people were encouraged to purchase the houses in America with low payments. The banks had been financing the balance of these loans at low interest rates. **These loans had been insured by the Federal agencies. These loans were then bundled up and sold in the open market as long term bonds by the banks and lending institutions. These were called sub-prime mortgage packages** which failed when borrowers could not honor their commitments of paying to their loans. Due to this reason, the banks and lending institutions could not honor their commitments to the bond holders, resulting in the collapse of the financial system in the United States.

In those days, borrowing money for homes, cars and other reasons was very easy. **People were financing up to 100% of the value of their properties.** The rules for verifications of income of the borrower and appraised values were not thoroughly verified. Everybody, including mortgage brokers, bankers, real estate agents and lawyers were making big money from the fees. They closed their eyes and let the system collapse. The property values were going up as speculators started bidding up, raising the prices, and refinancing them based on these new inflated prices. The consumer could not afford to make the payments and loans went into default.

The banks started closing on defaulted loans, flooding the market with the houses, resulting in drop in home values. The values dropped by more than 50% in

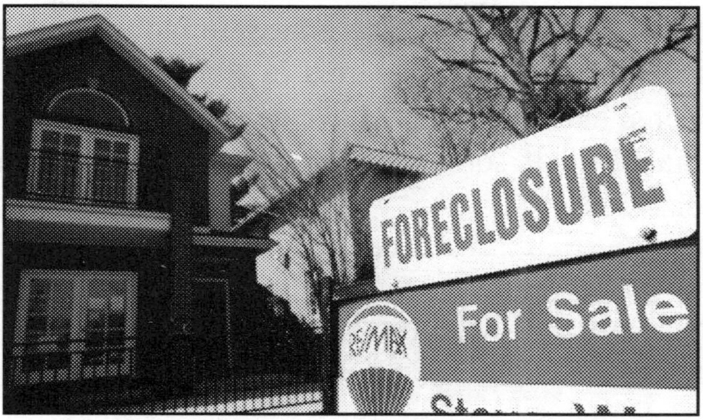

many cities. People just walked away from their homes as their equity became negative. I have known some houses, which were sold for more than $250,000 in 2005-2006 and by 2011 their values dropped to less than $100,000. Many of these houses had loans for more than $200,000.

While house values in America dropped by about 50%, in India, the values jumped up 2-3 folds during the

Commercial Construction

same period. **All of a sudden, Indian houses became more valuable and Indians became richer.** While vast majority of the houses in America have loans, it is reverse in India. There are about 10% houses in India which have loans. This trend has just started in last 10-15 years. It is considered unrespectable to have mortgage on your house in India. Even if somebody borrows money, it is done very discretely.

Bridge Construction in Agra India

In small cities in India, average houses are worth $150,000-$250,000. In the larger cities, it is $1,000,000 to $2,000,000. On top of it, Indians own substantial amount of gold of the world. It is very common to give gold as a gift in the Indian marriages. **People keep gold as security against any unforeseen circumstances or to support their children's education.**

In 2012, in an article in Globe and Mail, a Canadian National Newspaper, Stephanie Nolen wrote, that in Mumbai a small two room slum house, staked on top of each was listed for $43,000 dollars. In

Stephanie Nolen

Two-room shack, Mumbai slum.

Asking price: $43,000

Dharavi, the famous slum area, those shacks are selling for even higher prices. These are all paid up slum shacks, as there is no financing available to these slum houses. Even the poorest of the poor have equities in their houses in India. The house ownership in India is almost the same as in America. Indian's saving rates are one of the highest in the world.

As the housing industry was collapsing, the economy slowed down in America. The unemployment rose from 5% to 10%, Stock market lost about 50% of its value. Two of the three largest auto companies went bankrupt. Ford Motor Company's shares lost its values by more than 90%. It seemed the end of the economic domination of the United States in the world. In 2008, the Big 3 auto companies went to Washington to borrow money from the government.

Further, the real value of the Dollar is 1 dollar = 8 Indian rupees in terms of Purchasing Power, when compared with the minimum wage earners of both in New York and Mumbai.

Credit Cards

Credit cards are probably the largest culprit, causing people to go into financial calamities. Once people got the credit card in hand, their behavior becomes riddled with irrationalities.

The interest rates of 24% or more on the credit cards are very common. Many credit card companies allow the minimum payment to be as low that if you only make those payments it will take more than 10 yrs to pay off the entire principal amount. Further, the credit card companies charge other fees for late payment, over the limit charges, minimum usage charges, statement fees etc. The credit cards are one of the most lucrative businesses for the banks and other institutions. Average American has more than three credit cards and owed about $8,000 in 2009. Average student loan was $23,000. Credit cards have been introduced in India during last 10-15 years and less than 10% people have it. The student loans hardly exist.

Indian culture is to spend less than you earn, and save for the rainy day. The parents have taught this principle to the children from ages. Most have lived up to this principle and have peaceful and satisfied life. This has resulted in much lesser divorces and social problems for children and others.

Indians have much more equities in their houses than average Americans have, Indians have more gold and their saving rate is higher than that of Americans.

With more money in their hands, Indians give better education to their children, better medical facilities etc. which are part of the culture.

●

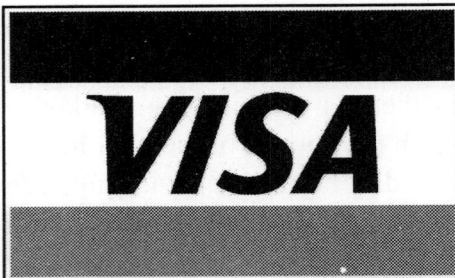

Chapter 13

Largest Democracy and Indian Personalities

Democracy is a type of government in which all eligible citizens have an equal say in the decisions that affect their lives.

Indian Parliament House

India is the world's largest democracy. India is run by a Parliament made up of two houses. These two houses are called the Lok Sabha (Lower House) and the Rajya Sabha (Upper House). The Parliament is located in India's capital, New Delhi. India has multi party system unlike USA, where it has two party system. The majority of the parties or coalition of the parties forms the government and their leader becomes the Prime Minister who runs the country with the approval of the Parliament.

President

Indian President's House

India's Head of the state is the President who is chosen by the both houses of the Parliament and state legislatures. The President is elected for a term of five years and serves only as a figurehead.

Supreme Court of India

The Supreme Court of India consists of 31 judges who sit in the Benches of 2-3, called Divisional Benches or in 5 or higher, called the Constitutional Benches. **The Constitution seeks to ensure the independence of Supreme Court Judges in various ways. Judges are generally appointed on the basis of seniority and not on political preference**

India Gate

India Gate is the national monument of India, located on Rajpath in New Delhi. Over 70,000 names of the soldiers are inscribed on the arch. It is a memorial of known and unknown soldiers who sacrificed their lives for the country.

Jawahar Lal Nehru

Nehru was the first Prime Minister of India after getting the independence in 1947. He is called the Architect of modern India. He was one of the greatest statesmen of the world. He was the Prime Minister for 17 years and died in 1964 at the age of 75.

Nehru's favorite Quotes:

—"Failure comes only when we forget our ideals and objectives and principles."

—"Ignorance is always afraid of change."

—"Action itself, so long as I am convinced that it is right action, gives me satisfaction."

—"Facts are facts and will not disappear on account of your likes."

—"Culture is the widening of the mind and of the spirit."

The world's largest democracy and second most populous country emerged as a major power in the 1990s. It's militarily is strong. It has major cultural influence in the world and is a fast-growing and powerful economy.

Sardar Vallabhabhai Patel

He was born in 1875 and was raised in the Gujarat. He was a very successful lawyer.

He was a social leader who played a leading role in the country's struggle for independence and was at the forefront of rebellions. He guided its integration into a united, independent Nation.

He was one of the leaders of the Indian National Congress and one of the founding fathers of the Republic of India.

Patel was the first Home Minister and Deputy Prime Minister of India. Patel organized relief for refugees in Punjab and Delhi. Patel took charge of the task to forge a united India from the British Colonial Provinces.

Indian Personalities

There are many great personalities who have changed the culture of India forever:

Dhirubhai Ambani

Dhiru Bhai Ambani built India's largest private sector company. Reliance is the first Indian company to feature in Forbes 500 list.

Dhirubhai Ambani was the most enterprising Indian entrepreneur. His life journey is reminiscent of the rags to riches story. He is remembered as the one who rewrote Indian corporate history and built a truly global corporate group.

Dhirubhai Ambani was born on December 28, 1932, at Chorwad, Gujarat. His father was a school teacher.

After doing his matriculation at the age of 16, Dhirubhai moved to Aden, Yemen. He worked there as a gas station attendant and as a clerk in an oil company. He returned to India in 1958 and set up a textile trading company.

Assisted by his two sons, Mukesh and Anil, Dhiru Bhai Ambani built India's largest private sector company, Reliance India Limited, from a scratch. Over time his business has diversified into a core specialization in petrochemicals with additional interests in telecommu-nications, information technology, energy, power, retail, textiles, infrastructure services, capital markets and logistics.

Dhirubhai Ambani is credited with shaping India's equity culture, attracting millions of retail investors in a market till then dominated by financial institutions. Dhirubhai revolutionized capital markets. From nothing, he generated billions of rupees in wealth for those who put their trust in his companies. His efforts helped create an 'equity cult' in the Indian capital market. With innovative instruments like the convertible debenture, Reliance quickly became a favorite of the stock market in the 1980s.

Dhirubhai Ambani was named the Indian Entrepreneur of the 20th Century by the Federation of Indian Chambers of Commerce and Industry (FICCI). A poll conducted by The Times of India in 2000 voted him "greatest creator of wealth in the century".

Dhirubhai Ambani died on July 6, 2002 at Mumbai.

Ratan Tata

Ratan Tata is one of the most well-known and respected Indian businessmen. He served as the Chairman of the Tata Group from 1991 till 2012. He is also a member of the prominent Tata family of Indian industrialists and philanthropists.

Ratan Tata was born on December 28, 1937 in Mumbai. He graduated with a degree in Architecture and Structural Engineering from Cornell University in 1962 and also did the Advanced Management Program from Harvard Business School in 1975.

In 1962, Ratan Tata began his career in the Tata group. In 1991, JRD Tata stepped down as the chairman of Tata Industries and named Ratan Tata as his successor. Under Ratan's stewardship, Tata Tea attained Tetley, Tata motors attained Jaguar Land Rover and Tata Steel attained Corus. These triumphs turned Tata from a large India-centric company into a global business with 65% revenues from abroad. He also contributed in the development of Indica and Nano.

Ratan Tata has also served in various organizations in India and abroad. He is a member of the Prime Minister's Council on Trade and Industry.

He was awarded the Padma Bhushan by the Government of India in January 2000. He serves on the Boards of several leading organizations, both in the public as well as the private sector in India.

On 28th December 2012, Ratan Tata retired from the Tata group. It also happened to be his 75th birthday. Ratan Tata is succeeded by Cyrus Mistry.

Ratan Tata's foreign affiliations include membership of the International Advisory Boards of the American International Group, J P Morgan Chase and Booz Allen Hamilton. He is also a member of the board of trustees of the R&D Corporation, University of Southern California and Cornell University. He is also a member of the Asia-Pacific advisory committee for the New York Stock Exchange. He received the Padma Bhushan in 2000 and Padma Vibhushan in 2008 and Lifetime Achievement Award awarded by Rockefeller Foundation.

Mukesh Ambani

Since time immemorial, we have witnessed the fact that sons inherit the legacy of their father, Dhirubhai Ambani. **Mukesh heads Reliance Industries, India's largest private sector company.** Born on April 19, 1957, Mukesh completed his Bachelor's in chemical engineering from the University of Mumbai, Department of Chemical Technology (UDCT). Then, he began his MBA program at Stanford Business School, but failed to finish it.

He joined Reliance in 1981 and initiated Reliance's backward integration from textiles into polyester fibers and further into petrochemicals. In the process, he directed the creation of 60 new, world-class manufacturing facilities involving diverse technologies that have raised Reliance's manufacturing capability from less than a million tonne to twelve million tonne per year. Mukesh Ambani led the creation of the World's largest grass roots petroleum refinery at Jamnagar, with a present capacity of 660,000 barrels per day.

Mukesh set up the largest information and

Communications technology in the world in the form of Reliance Infocom Limited, covering more than 1,100 towns and cities across India. He is steering a world-class offshore, deep water oil and gas exploration and production program. He has created a pan-India petroleum retail network involving 5,800 outlets.

The combined market capitalization of the four Mukesh Ambani group Companies—RIL, Reliance Petroleum (RPL), IPCL and Reliance Industrial Infrastructure Ltd (RIIL) has crossed the Rs 2,50,000 cr. ($45 Billion) mark. He has started a mega retail venture. He is married to Nita Ambani and has three children. His wife is also involved in numerous charitable and philanthropic activities. The Dhirubhai Ambani International School in Mumbai is a brainchild of Nita Ambani. His hard work is finally paying rich dividends and he deserves so.

Anand Mahindra

Anand Mahindra is the Managing Director and Vice Chairman of the Mahindra & Mahindra Group, which is amongst the top ten industrial houses in India.

This renowned group was established by his grandfather K.C. Mahindra in Ludhiana. Anand Mahindra is interested in educational issues and sports and thus, is a member of Harvard Business School - Asia-Pacific Advisory Board, Harvard Business School - **Member of the Board of Dean's Advisors, Harvard University Asia Centre - Advisory Committee, Asia Business Council, National Sports Development Fund (NSDF), Government of India - Council and Executive Committee, National Council of Applied Economic Research, National Institute of Bank Management, Pune - Governing Board. Apart from this, he is a big fan of football and plays tennis quite a lot too.**

In 1977, he pursued a graduate degree at the Harvard College, Cambridge, Massachusetts. He was a member of the Phoenix S.K. Club. In 1981, he finished his Masters in Business Administration from the Harvard Business School, Boston, Massachusetts. He is married to Anuradha Mahindra. The couple has two daughters.

In 1981, Anand Mahindra came back to India and joined the Mahindra Ugine Steel Company (MUSCO) as an Executive Assistant to the Finance Director. In 1989, he became the President of this leading group and this was when he expanded the company into the sectors of real estate development and hospitality. In 1991, he was assigned the duty of Deputy Managing Director of Mahindra & Mahindra Group. He took the responsibility as the Managing Director of the business in 1997 and became the Vice Chairman in 2003. Besides this, he was a Co-Promoter of Kotak Mahindra Finance Ltd., and transformed it into a bank in 2003. Kotak Mahindra Bank is now one of the leading banks in the private sector.

It was under Anand's management that his group

successfully set up global objectives and standards for achieving success. The company's acquisition activities include Satyam Computer Services in 2009, Reva Electric Vehicles in 2010 and Ssangyong Motor Company in 2010.

It has three assembly plants in the United States of America and has collaborated with international companies like Renault SA, Nissan and the International Truck and Engine Corporation, USA.

Anand has been the past President (2003-04) of the Confederation of Indian Industry and has also served the Automotive Research Association of India (ARAI) as its President. **Anand Mahindra is the Co-Founder of the Harvard Business School Association of India,** which is an association devoted to the advancement of professional management in India. He is also the Co-Chairperson of the World Economic Forum at Davos.

Mr. Anand is a Director of the National Stock Exchange of India Limited selected under the 'Public Representatives' category. Along with this, he is the Trustee of the K.C. Mahindra Education Trust, which offers scholarships to students and he is also on the Board of Governors of the Mahindra United World College of India. He is the Chairman of the National Safety Council of India and is the Founder Chairman of the Mumbai Festival, which began in 2005. This occasion was the first inclusive festival to celebrate the opulent cultural diversity of Maharashtra. Anand Mahindra is the Co-Chairman of the International Council of Asia Society, New York.

Anand Mahindra was honored as the Knight of the Order of Merit by the President of the French Republic in 2004 and also received the Rajiv Gandhi

Award for his outstanding contributions to the business field. It was in 2005, when he was awarded the Person of the Year award from Auto Monitor and the Leadership Award from the American India Foundation for the commitments to corporate social responsibility met by him and the Mahindra & Mahindra Group.

In 2006, he received the CNBC Asia Business Leader Award and the Ludhiana Management Association presented him with the Entrepreneur of the Year Award. In 2007. He has been entitled as the Business Leader of the Year (2008-2009) by the Economic Times Awards.

Anand Mahindra contributed $10 million to the Harvard University in the name of his mother, Indira Mahindra for supporting the Humanities Center.

Brijmohan Lall Munjal

Brijmohan Lall Munjal was born in 1923 at Kamalia, in unpartitioned Punjab, British India. Kamalia is now in Pakistan. He is from a simple middle-class Arora/Khatri family. After completing his formal education he worked at the Army Ordnance Factory, before moving his base to India after partition.

In 1944, when Brijmohan was 20, his family sensed partition, so **Brijmohan along with his elder brothers**

Dayanand Munjal, Satyanand Munjal and his younger brother Om Prakash Munjal came to India and settled in Amritsar. The brothers initially started a business with no money by supplying components to the manufacturers of bicycles in and around Amritsar. After the partition in 1947 the Munjal family completely shifted their base from Pakistan to Ludhiana.

At that point and still today, Ludhiana is an important destination for manufacturing and industry hub of bicycles and textiles. Slowly they expanded their distribution network and by early 1950s they were supplying components of bicycles throughout India.

In 1954 Hero Cycles Ltd moved up the value chain by making a shift from supplying to manufacturing. They started manufacturing handlebars, front forks and chains. In 1956, the Punjab Government issued tender notices for twelve new industrial licenses to make bicycles in Ludhiana. Brijmohan Lall Munjal and his brothers participated in the bid and won the contract. Hero Cycles was registered as a large-scale industrial unit.

In 1961 Rockman Cycles Industries was established to manufacture bicycle chains and hubs. Under his leadership Hero Cycles was the first company to export bicycles in large scale. In 1975 they had earned the distinction of largest bicycle manufactures in India. **By 1986 Hero Cycles Limited entered the Guinness Book of Records as the largest manufacturers of bicycles in the world.**

Before entering into a joint venture with Honda Motors, Dr. Munjal started the Majestic Auto Limited and started manufacturing Hero Majestic Moped. To manufacture motor cycles in 1984 the Hero Group started a joint venture with Hero Honda and established a plant at Dharuhera Haryana. **Hero Group expanded so big that by 2002 they had sold 86 million Bikes producing 16000 motorcycles a day, which is a world Guinness Book of Records.**

Different family members started other manufacturing companies in the course of time. **One of the companies, Munjal Showa, an auto parts company started by Brijmohan's older brother's (Sataynand's) son, Yogseh Munjal, is a $1.3 billion dollar company.** This company manufactures auto parts and supplies to many companies.

Today, Hero Cycles is one of the handful companies in India which can boast of a global scale of operations, not just in size, but also in technology. As the trade barriers between countries comes tumbling down, only companies with nothing short of world class production are expected to survive and **Hero Cycles, true to its leadership stature, has achieved a scale of production that can be matched by no other cycle producer in the world.**

Ambitions, beliefs, a strong culture of sensitivity and empathy are at the heart of the Hero Cycles brand.

Awards and recognition—

Awarded Businessman of the Year in 1994 by business magazine "Business India"

Received the National Award for outstanding contribution to the Development of Indian Small Scale Industry in 1995.

In 1999, featured in the Most Admired CEO List of the magazine, "Business Barons".

Received the Distinguished Entrepreneurship Award

from the PHD Chamber of Commerce and Industry in 1997, Xavier Labor Relations Institute (XLRI),

Conferred Sir Jehangir Ghandy Medal, for Industrial Peace in 2000. Featured as Earnest and Young Entrepreneur of the year in 2001.

Received the Lifetime Achievement award for "Management" from All India Management Association in 2003.

Banaras Hindu University, Varanasi conferred him with a Doctorate; degree of "Doctors of letters" Honoris Causa in October 2004.

Awarded "Padma Bhushan" in March 2005, for his contribution to the Trade and Industry in 2005.

Munjals have been supporting many charities and Arya Samaj, for many years and taking active part in the development of Indian culture.

Mahatma Satyanand, elder brother of Brijmohan, is a very spiritual man. He was the Managing Director of Hero Cycles Ludhiana. He started one Gurukul for girls in Ludhiana, where Vedas are taught along with modern education. He is running 8 schools and one B.Ed. College in Ludhiana. These schools produce the best results in the whole state of Punjab. One of the eight schools, is the only Hindi medium school in Punjab State. All the schools have regular Havans and spiritual education. He started 18 Arya Samajs in Ludhiana and revived several dormant Arya Samajs in Uttarakhand.

Mahatma Satyanand is the vice-president of D.A.V. Management and Arya Pratinidhi Sabha, Punjab. He is in the management committee of

Dayanand Medical College and Hospital, Ludhiana. He was the President of the Arya College, Ludhiana. He is the Chairman of Tankara (the birth place of Swami Dayanand Saraswati) Trust. He was conferred Mahatma by Swami Sarwanand of Dinanagar Punjab.

Mahashay Dharampal

Mahashian Di Hatti Limited is a distributor and exporter of ground spices and spice mixtures under the brand name MDH. It specializes in several unique traditional blends of spices suitable for different recipes. **It has grown in popularity all over India, and exports its products to several countries.** It is associated with Mahashay Chuni Lal Charitable Trust.

Mahashay Chuni Lal started the enterprise in Sialkot known as "Deggi Mirch Wale," after the name of one of their famous spice mixtures. After the partition of India, Mahashay Dharam Pal, the son of the founder, shifted to Delhi and opened up his shop at Ajmal Khan Road, Karol Bagh

The company has a capacity of producing 30 tonnes of packaged spices in a day. There are large fully automatic manufacturing plants at Delhi. It has now a network of over 1000 wholesalers and over 400,000 retail dealers in India. It was ranked 490th among the unlisted Indian companies in 2000-2001. MDH pioneered the marketing of powdered spice mixtures in handy attractive packages. It has been co-opted as member of several committees of the Bureau of Indian Standards. **In the last few years, the Exports Division of the company has started exporting the spices to several countries including UK, other European countries, Canada, United States, Japan and Switzerland.** They have now decided to foray into the ready-to-eat food segment as well. It is one of the best spices company not only in India but all over the world.

The MDH brand name is very well known throughout India. The products sold under the brand name include single spices (such as chili, coriander and turmeric) as well as blended spice mixtures. There are over 45 products available in over 100 different packages. The more famous ones are Chana Masala (for chickpeas), Sambar Masala (for Sambar), Kitchen King (for vegetables), Chunky Chaat Masala (for chaat),

MDH was awarded, the Institute of Trade and Industrial Development's ITID Quantity Excellence Award, 1994–95 Arch of Europe Gold Star for Excellence and Quality, 1999 and 2001.

The company has been involved in several charitable and social activities through its sister organization, Mahashay Chuni Lal Charitable Trust. **The trust operates a 250-bed hospital, a mobile hospital for slums, and four schools in New Delhi. Various social organizations can get need-based grants from the trust. It also brings out a monthly magazine Sandesh, focusing on traditional family values of India.**

A.K. Sud

Mayar Group has sales exceeding USD One Billion (INR 6000 cr.). At the helm of this trail-blazing group is Mr. A.K. Sud, Chairman and Managing Director of Mayar. He is supported by his sons, Ashit and Abhit Sud and by a workforce of sure-fire managers and committed staff. All are driven by a single philosophy...." The Best way to run a company is by serving the customer in more ways than one."

It was in 1948, just after Independence of India that Mayar Group was born in a small 10' x 12' shop, in a busy lane of old Delhi, Mayar came into being. Set up by the visionary industrialist, Late Shri Amar Nath Sud, this venture was named Mayar Traders Private Limited.

With over 6 decades, today companies forming pillars of the Mayar Group with its highly diversified Business portfolio and strong global footprints, it has become a conglomerate of international repute.

At Mayar, corporate vision is given a realistic touch with careful planning and forethought. It is a debt free company as it believes in expanding its interests by drawing on its own resources. From its corporate office in the beautiful Mayar Towers, the Group oversees **the activities of all its offices across the world - in Hong Kong, Malaysia, Singapore, Indonesia, Venezuela,**

Burma and Russia. Mayar group deals in many different products:

(*a*) **Publication Paper—**We acquired AO Volga in 1993 and were part owners till 2003 with a capacity of half million MT. During 2010-11, we sold 350000 MT of paper sourced from White Birch/SP Newsprint, North America/Canada, Shandong Huatai Paper Co. Ltd., China, SCA Laakirchen AG, Austria, Paper Corea, South Korea, Inforsa Chile, Aylesford Newsprint U.K. to our customers. We are the exclusive supplier of these manufacturers for the Indian market.

(*b*) **Timber—**We are the largest exporter of Timber logs to India, Bangladesh, Vietnam and Middle East. The company has its own sourcing net work and owns forest concession in Myanmar, Malaysia and New Zealand.

(*c*) **Beans and Pulses—**We are the leading importers of Agro products from various countries.

(*d*) **Shipping—**The company owns 6 midsized log carriers DWT 30000 to 40000 tons. The ships are deployed for captive use.

(*e*) **Hospitality—**We are in the wellness business and own the famous brands Amatrra Spa and Three Graces. We are opening shortly Destination Resorts in Gurgaon, Goa and Utrakhand.

(*f*) **Infrastructure—**The company is developing a Biotechnology SEZ in Gurgaon, NCR under the name Mayar Biotech.

Mayar Group supports many charities. One of them is Amar Eye Centre & Research Foundation, conveniently located in east Delhi and serves the rich

and the poor with equal dedication.

The main objective of this foundation is to make available the latest diagnostic and operative facilities at a reasonable cost. Which is why Mayar has equipped it with the latest imported equipment like operative microscopes, slit lamps, synaptophore, applanation tono meters, computerized perimetry and state of the art eye testing and ultra sound equipment.

With a panel of specialists and highly qualified and dedicated personnel, the center envisages to spearhead a revolution in quality eye care for all in the country.

Lakshmi Mittal

Lakshmi Niwas Mittal (born 15 June 1950) is an England-based Indian steel magnate. He is the chairman and CEO of Arcelor Mittal, the world's largest steelmaking company.

Mittal is the richest man of Asian descent. He was ranked the sixth richest person in the world by Forbes in 2011. He is in the "Most Powerful People" list for 2012. His daughter Vanisha Mittal's wedding was the second most expensive in recorded history.

Mittal has been a member of the Board of Directors of Goldman Sachs since 2008, and is also member of the board of directors of the European Aeronautic Defense and Space Company. He sits on the World Steel Association's executive committee, and is a member of the Indian Prime Minister's Global Advisory Council, the World Economic Forum's International Business Council, and the Presidential International Advisory Board of Mozambique. He also sits on the advisory board of Northwestern University's Kellogg School of Management in the United States and is a member of the board of trustees of the Cleveland Clinic.

In 2006 The Sunday Times named him "Business Person of 2006", the Financial Times named him "Person of the Year", and Time magazine named him "International Newsmaker of the Year 2006." In 2007, Time magazine included him in their "100 most influential persons in the world."

Mittal, set up Mittal Champions Trust with $9 million to support 10 Indian athletes with world-beating potential. Arcelor Mittal also financed the construction of Arcelor Mittal Orbit for 2012 Summer Olympics.

In 2012, the Lakshmi Niwas Mittal and Usha Mittal Foundation and the Government of Rajasthan partnered together to establish a university, the LNM Institute of Information Technology (LNMIIT) in Jaipur as an autonomous non-profit organization.

In 2009, the Foundation along with Bharatiya Vidya Bhavan founded the Usha Lakshmi Mittal Institute of Management in New Delhi.

SNDT Women's University renamed the Institute of Technology for Women(ITW) as Usha Mittal Institute of Technology after a large donation from the Lakshmi Niwas Mittal Foundation.

Narayana Murthy

Narayana Murthy is an Indian businessman and co-founder of Infosys. Murthy started Infosys in 1981 and served as its CEO from 1981 to 2002. From 2002 to 2011, he served as the Chairman. In 2011, he stepped down from the Board and became Chairman Emeritus.

Fortune magazine has listed Infosys co-founder NR Narayana Murthy among the 12 "greatest entrepreneurs of our time" along with Apple's late chief Steve Jobs, Microsoft founder Bill Gates and Facebook CEO, Mark Zuckerberg.

"The outsourcer" Murthy, who has been ranked tenth, "proved that India could compete with the world by taking on the software development work that had long been the province of the West," the US magazine said.

The "visionary founder" of Infosys, has built "one of the largest companies in India, helping to transform that economy and put it on the world stage"

His accomplishments in both business and charitable endeavors are remarkable. Most impressive are his humility as an influential entrepreneur and philanthropist. Narayana Murthy, was announced as the recipient of the 2012 James C. Morgan Global Humanitarian Award at an event at the Tech Museum in San Jose, California. In expressing his gratitude for the award, he spoke of philanthropy as bringing justice and equity to the world and making the planet more peaceful and harmonious.

Sudha Murthy wife of Narayana Murthy is an Indian social worker and author. She is the chairperson of the Infosys Foundation and member of public health care initiatives of the Gates Foundation. She has established several orphanages, participated in rural development efforts, and supported the movement to provide all government schools in Karnataka with computer and library facilities.

In 2006, Murthy was awarded the Padma Shri, the fourth highest-ranking civilian award from the Government of India, and received an honorary doctorate for her contributions in the spheres of social work, philanthropy, and education.

Sunil Mittal

Sunil Mittal was born in Ludhiana. His father, Sat Pal Mittal, had been the Member of Parliament (M.P.) from Ludhiana. He graduated in 1976 from Punjab University, Chandigarh, with a Bachelor of Arts and Science.

A first generation entrepreneur, Mittal started his first business in April 1976 at the age of 18, with a capital investment of INR20,000 (US$364) borrowed from his father. His first business was to make crankshafts for local bicycle manufacturers.

In 1980, he along with his brothers Rakesh, Rajan started an Import Enterprise named Bharti Overseas Trading Company. He sold his bicycle parts and yarn factories and moved to Mumbai.

In 1981, he imported thousands of Suzuki Motors's portable electric-power generators from Japan. The import of generators was suddenly banned by the then Indian Government. Licenses to manufacture generators in India were issued to two companies.

In 1984, he started assembling push-button phones in India. Bharti Telecom Limited (BTL) was incorporated and entered into a technical tie up with Siemens AG of Germany for manufacture of electronic push button phones. **By the early 1990s, Mittal was making fax machines, cordless phones and other telecom gear. Mittal says,** "In 1983, the government imposed a ban on the import of gensets. I was out of business overnight. Everything I was doing came to a screeching halt. I was in trouble. I noticed the popularity of the push-button phone —something which India hadn't seen then. We were still using those rotary dials with no speed dials or redials. I sensed my chance and embraced the telecom business."

In 1992, he successfully bid for one of the four mobile phone network licenses auctioned in India. One of the conditions for the Delhi cellular license was that the bidders have some experience as a telecom operator. So,

Mittal clinched a deal with the French telecom group Vivendi.

He was one of the first Indian entrepreneurs to identify the mobile telecom business as a major growth area. His plans were finally approved in 1994 and he launched services in Delhi in 1995, when Bharti Cellular Limited (BCL) was formed to offer cellular services under the brand name AirTel. Within a few years Bharti became the first telecom company to cross the 2-million mobile subscriber mark.

In November 2006, he struck a joint venture deal with Wal-Mart, the US retail giant, to start a number of retail stores across India.

Dr. S. K. Maini

Dr. S. K. Maini, a well known industrialist, produced India's first electric car, Reva. Since 1973, he has started many industries including precision tools, material handling equipment, golf cart manufacturing and all terrain vehicles used for the army, employing thousands of people.

Dr. Maini's philiosophy of Zero

It is nothing more complicated than a Circle—And yet in that symbol is a world of meaning. By the way it places itself, it can multiply any number to dizzying heights.

Zero is the cosmic order of things eternally in motion—yet ever unchanging, it is not about nothingness—it is about infinity, it is not about failure—it is about perfection beyond standards.

We have developed the zero principle as our working philosophy.

We aim to deliver Zero Defect Products with Zero Time Delay, Zero Excuses and Zero Complaints.

We achieve this through Zero Wastage, Zero Compromise and Zero Inefficiency. We believe in Zero Pollution.

And Zero is our Inspiration!

After his three sons, Sandeep, Gautam and Chaten took over the business. Dr. Maini started Gramothan Foundation under which he took over to train the people of 22 villages of India to provide them with clean water and also developing hygienic values among them. He is also helping them to become entrepreneurs. Dr. S. K. Maini, was born in Ludhiana.

The primary object of Gramothan is to improve the quality life of Tribal and Rural India. 84% of the population of the rural India currently (600 million) are poor. Gramothan Foundation, by initiating variety of actions will target for eliminating poor from rural India in the shortest possible time not exceeding 10 years (2019).

The major emphasis while improving the quality of life will be through involvement of the villagers themselves. Gramothan Foundation will only teach them, help them, train them and facilitate them in improving the productivity of their land by better farming methods of their cattle by more effective usage of wastages, of their spare time by providing skills through training and thereafter work. The emphasis will be for villages to be self sufficient as far as possible individually and certainly when considered them in small clusters.

Gramothan Foundation actions in alleviating poverty and improving the quality of life in Rural India will also result in reducing the movement of rural people from villages to cities.

Each village will have a samithi (Committee) who would take active part in the progress of the village. Trained personnel will be stationed in every village who with the help of Gram samithi members shall implement various schemes in the field of basic education, hygiene and health, farming and non-farming work including vermi compost, phenyl from Gomutra etc. Special emphasis will be given on utilization of wastages currently prevalent in the villages now. These also include cow dung, cow urine and even human urine and human waste.

Dr. Maini believes "The society which Scorns excellence in plumbing because plumbing is a humble activity and tolerates shoddiness in philosophy because it is an exalted activity will have neither good plumbing nor good philosophy neither its pipes nor its theories will hold water."

Dr. Maini wrote the world famous book about the visionary of modern India, the Biography of "Madan Mohan Malaviya" which was launched by the Prime Minister of India, Manmohan Singh, in December of 2011. He is also the Managing Trustee of the Mahamana Malaviyaji Trust, Banglore.

Dr. Maini pursued his Mechanical Engineering from Banaras Hindu University and was awarded an Honorary Doctorate in Technology from very prestigious, Lougborough University, England. He also received the distinguished "IT-BHU Alumni Life Time Achievement Award" in 2009.

Dr. Maini along with his brothers, a very distinguished professor of Punjab University, Dr. D P Maini, Air Force Commander Dr. S P Maini and Wing Commander Madan Mohan Maini are one of the most dedicated Indians.

Karam Chand Thapar

Karam Chand Thapar (born in 1900) was the founder of the Thapar Group of companies. He was originally from Punjab. He started his career in 1920 as a coal trader in Calcutta, and built up the family fortune through Karam

Chand Thapar and Bros. He then started JCT Limited that is into textiles as well as molasses and alcohol. He also took over the Oriental Bank of Commerce, and ventured into paper manufacturing with the Ballarpur Industries Limited. K C Thapar established Karam Chand Thapar & Bros Ltd.

In 1920, he set out for Calcutta, the Erstwhile Capital of India, where he began to establish contacts with other Indian businessmen with the aim of convincing them to rally against the British stranglehold over coal production and distribution in India. That same year, he started a successful coal distribution business based out of Calcutta. As a leader, Karam Chand managed to consolidate a diverse group of investors and contractors, and incorporate them into his coal distribution network. He then began to rapidly acquire and develop coal mines in the states of Bihar, West Bengal, Madhya Pradesh and Maharashtra.

Karam Chand did not focus on coal alone but also ventured into other fields like paper, textiles, chemicals, sugar as well as banking (Oriental Bank of Commerce) and insurance (United Indian Insurance). In 1929, the flagship parent company of the Thapar Group "the Group", Karam Chand Thapar & Bros. Ltd., was formed. In the course of time, various companies owned and/or managed by Karam Chand were brought under its umbrella.

In 1956 he started the Thapar Institute of Engineering and Tech. In 1985 the college was made a Deemed University and renamed as Thapar University.

Aamir Khan

Aamir Khan, born on 14 March 1965, is an Indian film actor, director and producer. He is the recipient of many awards, including 4 National Film Awards and 7 Filmfare Awards, and was honored by the Government of India with the Padma Shri and the Padma Bhushan.

Khan first appeared on screen as a child actor in the film Yaadon Ki Baaraat and he began a full-time career in films with a leading role in the highly successful Qayamat Se Qayamat Tak. **He established himself as a leading actor of Hindi cinema in the 1990s by appearing in several commercially successful films.** He was also noted for playing against type in the critically acclaimed Canadian-Indian film Earth.

In 2001, Khan started a production company, whose first release, Lagaan, was nominated for the Academy Award for Best Foreign Language Film and earned him a National Film Award for Best Popular Film and two more Filmfare Awards.

He emphasized on the importance of small towns in the film industry stating, that the film makers don't understand small town India. This experience of reaching out to 'regional India' was extended in his debut TV show Satyamev Jayate. **In 2011, Khan was appointed National Brand Ambassador of UNICEF to promote**

child nutrition. He is a part of the government organized IEC campaign to raise awareness about malnutrition.

Aamir started Satyamev Jayate, a show dealing with social issues of the society. The concept of the show is true to its purpose that is, creating social awareness among common people. The show is about interacting with the common man of India, deliberating with them the issues connected with the live issues in India. He hopes that audience would bring solutions by their own understanding and paradigm shifts connected with the social issues. The themes selected include medical malpractice, child sexual abuse, honor killings, domestic violence, alcoholism, plight of senior citizens and cleanliness etc., besides covering practical issues like water crisis and corruption.

Aamir is making a difference in every Indian's life.

Govind Dholakia

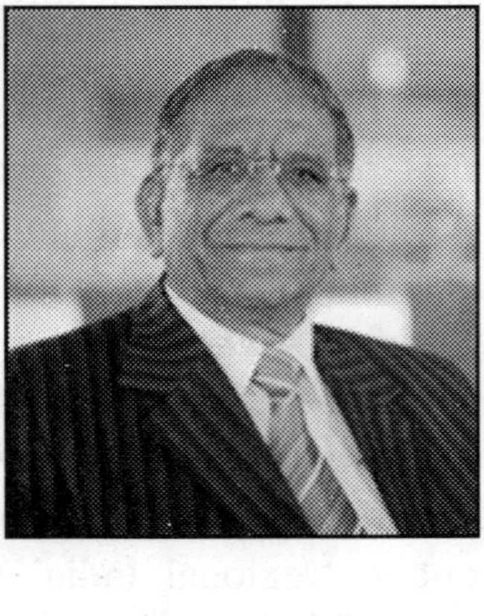

Govind Dholakia became the chairman of SRK in 1964 after dedicating his passion and hard work for diamonds. SRK - one of the leading diamond manufacturing unit in Surat, Gujarat (India) includes brands such as D.Goldi, A.Goldi, V.Goldi, R.Goldi, S.Goldi, J.Goldi Jewel Goldi (JGI) & The Jewellery Co. (TJC)

Govind Dholakia was born on 7 November, 1947 in

a small village of Dudhala, Amreli (District in Gujarat) in one of the petty joint Gujarati family comprised of total 40 members.

Govind Dholakia is lovingly known as Govindkaka. At the age of 13 he went to Surat and started working as a diamond cutter. He worked with strong dedication, day and night. He went through several hardships and struggles but was committed and always loved his work.

In 1970, with an investment of Rs.5000 ($100), his vision came in to existence and he started a small business with two partners. He started his 1st Import Export operation in 1977 in the name of Shree Ramkrishna Export.

In 1995 all partners decided to diversify and parted to set up their own diamond manufacturing firms.

In 1997 Govind Dholakia expanded his horizon and tied up with a marketing affiliate - 'D. GOLDI in Antwerp, Belgium to cater to the European market.

He received several awards & recognition in the industry for his outstanding contribution in the industry. His hunger for growth did not stop there.

In 2011 Govind Dholakia took SRK to newer heights by inaugurating one of the largest factories - 'SRK Empire' in the industry with all the latest technology and machines. His beautiful factory is one of the best examples in the industry. With this, his dream came true, and today he is living with his dream SRK.

Today, Shree Ramkrishna Exports Pvt. Ltd (SRK) is a half billion dollar company having an annual turnover of Rs.3500 cr.

SRK is one of the world's leading diamonds manufacturing company in Industry having 50 years of legendry experience & strong loyal customer base.

Govind Dholakia's life is a source of inspiration to many in the industry. With no higher educational degrees, and no forefathers in this business, he single-handedly established such a gigantic brand – SRK. He believes that 'Problem is Progress'.

"Positivity and strong will power is his key for success. There is no space for negative feelings."

Apart from diamonds, His passion is philanthropy and serving people. He believes in spreading smiles over miles. Social Service is a part and parcel of his life. He has built and maintained several charitable trusts under his supervision.

"Shree Ramkrishna Charitable Trust" was established by Govind Dholakia in the year 1988 at Surat. It provides free medical facilities and treatment to the needy people and another medical center "Matrushri Nanduba Medical Center" has also been operating.

He took special interest in educating girl child. He started with 'Godhani Girls School' in loving memory of his partner Virji Godhani at Surat. SRK is also affiliated with many other educational Institutes.

Laxamipati Sarees, Surat

Today, Shri Govind Sarawagi has become a well established renowned name in the famous Textile Market of Asia. With his hard work, honesty, determination and true duty sense, he has expanded his business beyond India, in foreign countries and proved with a symbolic recognition that:

> "Where there is strong light of Manlihood,
> Exists there a stream of advanced life."

"Laxmipati Sarees" is a brand name today. Fully confident with closed eyes, when businessmen exhibit this brand in their shops, then with the same confidence, customers also take away this brand product sarees to their house.

In 1984, with the assistance of three employees, **Shri Govindji Sarawagi** took a shop on rent in Surat Textile Market and started his dream textile business. For two years Shri Sarawagi himself expanded the business. Following the Indian tradition **Sanjay Sarawagi,** the eldest son of Shri Govindji started contributing the work of his father in 1986. Before stepping into this field, Sanjay gained full experience in weaving field. Thereby with his interest and experience and with the help of his two brothers, **Manoj** and **Rakesh,** the business started progressing. With three brothers working together, the company's turnover increased from 40 cr. to over 270 cr. in few years. The company has the largest printing machine in Asia Pacific with 24 colour printing machine and has over 100 shops all over India.

"To deliver innovative and quality product to our customer by following a progressive, purist and eco-friendly approach" is the motto of the company. Pollution control measures, energy and water saving measures are taken good care at Laxamipati.

Govind Prasad Sarawagi is well known for his social

work, providing medical facilities at Siadhi Vinayak Hospital, Surat at very nominal cost. Sri Govind Prasad Sarawagi Charitable Trust supports many social works. Shri Govind Prasad Sarawagi has been awarded, "Indira Gandhi Priyadarshini Award" for social work.

Geeta Shroff

Mrs. Geeta Deepak Shroff is a woman with many talents. A Social worker who has campaigned various woman's and family causes, made contributions through Education and organised events. She gives her Honorary Services (Day n Night also) in Religious, Social, Judicial, Police, Surat Mahanagar Palika, Veer Narmad South Gujarat University, Income Tax Dept., Slum People, Mentally Challenged Organization, Schools, Adivasi Area, Ashram Shala & many more. She completed her graduation after 18 years of marriage and started L.L.B. She has helped to setup a Family Court in Surat & giving conciliation services with trained team. She is a Panel Member of the Consumer Dispute Redressal Forum, Surat.

She is the President of NGO ANIS (Aapmatyu Nivaran Sahay). From 1999 till date the ANIS team gives honorary services at woman's and other all Police Station of Surat. Under her guidance, aggrieved families were saved from domestic violence, harassment and separating into nuclear families. Along with the support of Surat Channel 'Sahiyar' the T.V. serial, she hosted and scripted more than 80 episodes to motivate women to discuss their issues and even succeeded to save many women from suicide. These efforts helped to bridge the gap between the Police and Women of the city.

Since 2003 she has been a part of "Housewives Training Workshops" organized by "Umiya Parivar Trust" where women were educated to prevent sexual and domestic harassment. She also arranged seminar training the Police on effective investigation for violence perpetuated on women. She has even worked as a counselor at Family Courts and District Courts to stop family separations.

In 2006 the "Beti Bachao Abhiyaan" was executed under her guidance. She along with Rinky Bhatacharya Women Activist (Mumbai) and Prem Sharda, Vice Chancellor organized discussion forums on Documentary Film "Behind the Closed Door". After the 2009 Gang-Rape case, she took program initiative 'Josh bhi he, Hosh bhi hai' with Limca Book Record Holder Dr Raj Shetty and till today with Pamir Shah (Women Against Rape and Domestic Abuses Trainer), she trained lakhs of girls Self-Defense.

By 2012-2013 she initiated SAAR 'Surat Acts Against Rape' movement and 'Beti Swa-Shakti Karan' (self-empowerment).

She organized the first vocational camp for children 'Bhaudik Vikas Sankul' and organised elocution and discussions in various schools on

'Samjho Samasya Balko ni' & coordinator of " Parenting For Peace" by IGP Hasmukh Patel (IPS).

She is an Advisory committee Member of India's first Children University in Gandhinagar Gujarat. For youth 'Yuva Talim Shivir' is an activity conducted to educate and give awareness on 'Maro Remote Mara Haath Maa' & National Youth Conclave at Surat. & Member of Anti Sexual Harressment Cell n Anti Ragging Cell n Women Cell in leading companies, Goverment Department etc. also Visitors Board Member in Central Jail of Surat.

For the first time in Surat, a Wedding Exhibition was organized by her and got recognized at an international level. She also organized a Kids Carnival. Sankalpkar of "Narkesari Narendra Modi" book. Plus she has been the initiator and producer of 'Hun Surat' a documentary on Surat & "Masumiyat Apna Hathma" " Beti Apki Hamari" on rape of minor girls to be shown globally.

From 2005 she served as a trustee and coordinator for 'Traffic Education Trust' 1st time in India with public participation which started in other cities like Ahmedabad, Vadodara, Rajkot etc, on the suggestion of the Honourable Chief Minister. She tried to make Surat's Family Court ideal by organizing Yoga, Children Room, library, healing music and motivational programs. In 2010, she played a significant role being a part of 'Swarnim Gujarat, Vanchi Gujarat' (Government of Gujarat).

She has been involved in various social activities like Blood Donation Camps, Eye and Dental Shivir, to prevent Cancer Awareness Programs and many more. She has also played a role as an environmentalist by being a part of 'Prayaas Sanstha' that focuses on growing more trees and saving birds to protect nature.

Undoubtedly Mrs Geeta Deepak Shroff's contribution to society has helped its betterment. Her entrepreneurial skills and hardworking never say die attitude has helped society deal with new age problems like joint families separating into nuclear ones, problems within a marriage, rape etc. She is not just a social worker but entrepreneur, producer, writer, speaker as well as a daughter-in-law, a wife and a mother of two sons and daughter in law.

Rajni Bector

Rajni Bector is the Founder and Chairperson of Cremica Group of Companies. She was born in Karachi on June 2nd 1941 to Rai Sahib Divan Chand Talwar, Chief of Accounts in Erstwhile, India. Rajni was married to Sh. Dharamvir Bector at a very tender age into a well known business family of Ludhiana.

Rajni has baked her success story working against the odds. A cooking aficionado, she started making ice-creams and baking cakes more as a hobby. She would try new recipes and invite friends and relatives to savor her cooking skills. With no time, the word spread and she started getting catering orders. That was the time when her dream of becoming an entrepreneur was born.

It was a difficult time as in those days it was taboo for women from elite Punjabi families to work. Despite peer pressure, she prepared salads, sweet dishes and puddings for 2000 people for a friend's wedding, and that too with little help. This was a huge success which led to the establishment of the first unit in the annexes of the house with no worker and only an ice-cream churner worth Rs. 300, which soon expanded to many other units all over India within a short span of two decades. Today, Ludhiana-based Cremica Group sales are Rs. 650 cr. and the Group is valued at over Rs. 700 cr.

Well known as the doyenne of food processing industry in North India, Rajni Bector has been nurturing the company since 1979. Rajni has included a number of products under fold today include breads, biscuits, sauces, gravies, ice-creams and condiments. **Company is also a key supplier to McDonald's, ITC, Cadbury, HUL, Big Bazzar, Spencers, Sodexo, Taj Group, Indian Army, Jet Airways, Indian Airlines, Railways, Barrista, Cafe Coffee Day, Piza Hut, Dominos and Papa John in the domestic and international market.**

Awards and Honours—

Business woman of the year award given by PHDCCI, presented by the Hon'ble President of India, Shri Abdul Kalam in 2005.

Business woman of the year award by SIDBI presented by Shri Pranab Mukherjee Finance

Minister (current President of India), Govt of India in 2010.

Awarded by FICCI for Business and Entrepreneurship by Mrs. Shelia Dixit, Chief Minister of Delhi in 2009

PHDCCI Award by Capt. Amrinder Singh, Chief Minister of Punjab in 2005

For social service awarded by Shri Jagjivan Ram, Defense Minister India in 1966

Awarded by Giani Zail Singh, then Chief Minister of Punjab (ex-President of India), for leading service projects in 1979

Rajni Bector also worked as a strong social activist committed to the social causes like Women Empower-ment, Rural development, Generation of Employment opportunities for the backward and unemployed. She has employed and trained 1500 women to stand on their own feet. Mrs. Bectors services have been recognized at national and international level. In an endeavor to generate more employment opportunities **Cremica currently have 4000 direct employees and 1000 indirect employees.**

As the first chairperson of the Lioness Club of North India, organized various blood donation camps, free eye camps and medical camps.

Organized camps to provide artificial limbs and treatments to needy and handicapped. She is also the driving force behind NGO called Ek Prayas, an institute for Special Children.

Dr. Adlakha

Born on 5th November, 1936, he migrated from West Pakistan in Aug, 1947. **He completed Master's in Surgery with ENT Specialty in a record time of two years, while doing night duty as Casualty Medical Officer, V.J. Hospital, Amritsar. He taught in Medical College, Amritsar from 1968 to 1978. He got married with Dr. Sharda Adlakha MBBS, DGO in 1968. He has two children Shivalika and Sahil.** He started his own hospital called "Adlakha Hospital", Race Course Road, Amritsar. While working in hospital, he held about hundred free ENT and Gyne camps all over rural areas of Punjab.

Adlakha Hospital is a pioneer in starting first Ultra Sound Diagnostics Centre in Amritsar and establishing Test Tube Baby Project and Gyne-Endoscopy surgery center in collaborating with Dr. Rakesh Sinha from Mumbai.

Dr. Adlakha was the President of Indian Medical Association, Amritsar branch for the year 1980-1981. Also served as President of Service Club, Ram Bagh Gardens, Amritsar for two and a half years. Dr. Adlakha has written various articles on social issues published in Punjabi Tribune, Chandigarh. Dr. Adlakha promoted the concept of zero garbage places and gave lectures on Municipal Solid Waste Management in various institutes of Amritsar. These days he is busy in promoting hearing aid use in deaf people and holding various ear check-up camps in various parts of Punjab.

Girish Khosla

A highly educated and noble well known Dada (Grand Father), which more than 200 orphans call him, after he along with a highly dedicated person, Acharya Vachonidhi started a five star like institution for those orphans of Gujrat's earthquake of 2001. They started with one child and grew them to hundreds, raising them from a small place to a four acres land, Jeevan Prabhat, a five star like hotel facilities in Gandhidham, Gujrat.

Rarely, you will find a place in the world, where orphans are being raised in like an upper middle class facilities with real human values being engraved in the children's minds. Every day, they are sent to schools in the modern yellow buses in uniforms and evening activities in their two acres extremely well landscaped park (probably, better than 90% parks in America), Mr. Khosla from Michigan, USA, and Mr. Vachonidhi from Gujarat, India, has set an example to the world that how people from two different countries, can change the lives of hundreds of helpless, orphan children, which will eventually bring peace and prosperity to the world.

His wife, Suman's and son, Bhuvnesh's dedications are unparalleled to make success for Mr. Khosla's mission to bring peace in the world. Mr. Khosla is also the founder and organizer of Arya Sammalen and recently celebrated 23rd annual function in Toronto, Canada. He also publishes monthly magazine, Navrang Times, from Michigan which is distributed all over the world.

Dr. Balvir Acharya

Dr Balvir Acharya was born on 23rd May, 1952 in Fazalpur (Sundar Nagar) Distt. Baghpat. U.P. He received his early education (Shastri and Acharya) from Gurukul Jhajjar, Distt. Jhajjar, Haryana. **He passed his Master's degree (M.A. Veda & Sanskrita) from Gurukul Kangri University, Haridwar (Uttarakhand). He did his Ph.D. from Garhwal University Shrinagar (Uttarakhand) and D. Litt. from Agra university (U.P).**

Apart from the fact that he has, to his credit, many publications, he combines admirably, the twin qualities of an effective, incisive teacher and an erudite reader. He is a learned Sanskrit scholar and is well versed in Vedic literature. He is an avowed preceptor/Preacher of Vedic Hindu culture, Religion and Philosophy. He has over a period of time, gained expertise in curing chronic maladies with the help of Yogic, Acupressure and Su-jok therapy. His wholehearted interest in social activities is by no means less laudatory.

He has recently retired from professorship in the Department of Sanskrit, Maharshi Dayanand University, Rohtak, Haryana, India. **He has been a member of University Academic Council, Chairperson of Department of Sanskrit, Chairperson of Maharshi Dayanand Saraswati chair and various other Academic Bodies.** He has also been a member of the Sahitya Academy (National Academy of Letters), set up by the Govt. of India to work actively for the development and promotion of Indian literature.

Under his guidance thirty students did Ph.D. and forty students did M.Phil.

Vachonidhi Acharya

A noble person, who left his prestigious and well paid job as Bank Manager in India, after he saw the disaster of the earth quake of Gujarat in 2001. It happened in his hometown of Gandhidham, got the members of his local Arya Samaj to join him. They took the orphans to their facilities until the number grew to more than 50, after which they built the beautiful, Jeevan Prabhat.

Mr. Vachonidhi did not quit there, he started D.A.V. school for more than 1200 students and now about to start a vocational school on the newly acquired 13 acres land in Gandhidham to train people in different trades, for them to be prepared for new world's challenges. He and his wife, Suman, are doing all these services without any compensation and rather contribute every year to the cause of improving lives of helpless. Their two boys, Manasavi and Tanmay, are equally helping the orphans and others.

Pandit Ravi Shankar

Ravi Shankar was born on 7 April 1920 in Varanasi, India. He was the youngest of seven brothers.

At the age of ten, after spending his first decade in Varanasi, Shankar went to Paris with the dance group of his brother, choreographer, Uday Shankar. By the age of 13 he had become a member of the group, accompanied its members on tour and learned to dance and play various Indian instruments. Uday's dance group toured Europe and the United States of America in the early to mid-1930s and Shankar learned French, discovered Western classical music, jazz, cinema and became acquainted with Western custom.

In 1956 he toured to the United Kingdom, Germany,

and the United States. He played for smaller audiences and educated them about Indian music, incorporating ragas from the South Indian Carnatic music in his performances, and recorded his first LP album Three Ragas in London, released in 1956. In 1958, Shankar participated in the celebrations of the tenth anniversary of the United Nations and UNESCO music festival in Paris. From 1961, he toured Europe, the United States, and Australia, and became the first Indian to compose music for non-Indian films.

Shankar befriended Richard Bock, founder of World Pacific Records, on his first American tour and recorded most of his albums in the 1950s and 1960s for Bock's label. The Byrds recorded at the same studio and heard Shankar's music, which led them to incorporate some of its elements in theirs, introducing the genre to their friend George Harrison of The Beatles. Harrison became interested in Indian classical music, bought a sitar and used it to record the song "Norwegian Wood (This Bird Has Flown)". This led to Indian music being used by other musicians and created the raga rock trend.

Harrison met Shankar in London in 1966 and visited India for six weeks to study sitar under Shankar in Srinagar. During the visit, a documentary film about Shankar named Raga was shot by Howard Worth, and released in 1971. Shankar's association with Harrison greatly increased Shankar's popularity and Ken Hunt of Allmusic would state that Shankar had become "the most famous Indian musician on the planet" by 1966.

During the 1970s, Shankar and Harrison worked together again, recording Shankar Family & Friends in

1973 and touring North America the following year to a mixed response after Shankar had toured Europe with the Harrison-sponsored Music Festival from India.

He served as a member of the Rajya Sabha, the upper chamber of the Parliament of India, from 12 May 1986 to 11 May 1992, after being nominated by Indian Prime Minister Rajiv Gandhi.

He received the music award of the UNESCO International Music Council in 1975, three Grammy Awards, and was nominated for an Academy Award. Shankar was awarded honorary degrees from universities in India and the United States

Shankar was a Hindu and a vegetarian. He wore a large diamond ring which he said was ''manifested'' by Sathya Sai Baba. He lived with Sukanya in Encinitas, California.

Satinder Mahajan

Mr. Mahajan took a bigger responsibility after retiring as bank manager of a very prestigious bank. Many of his colleagues have taken to travel or other avenues, but not Mr. Mahajan. He looked around and saw many older people suffering from personal and health problems in Ludhiana. He took the lead and with a small group of people started medical clinics, teaching hygienic values and interaction among them.

Mr. Mahajan is a visionary and figured out that the seniors need a permanent place of their own. Recently, he arranged a charity event, where many leaders attended along with the public and raised

huge amount of funds for a permanent place to build for seniors.

He is very much loved in the city. Even the Mayor, Police Commissioner and other top government officials help and appreciate his efforts for improving the lives of local senior citizens.

Vijay Deora

I have rarely seen a more dedicated Principal of a school than Mr. Vijay Deora with four Master's degrees and taking care of more than 1800 students of Arya Higher Secondary School, a very famous school of its time in Ludhiana, Punjab.

Mr. Deora gets involved with all the activities of the children's well being, arranging scholarships, books, clothing and many more for hundreds who needed.

Hiralal Jain

One of the greatest men in Ludhiana, the Samrat Rattan of Jain Community, Mr. Hira Lal Jain is one of the most dedicated persons in India.

He is the founder and Director of Mahavir International and General Secretary of Bhagwan Mahavir 2600th Janam Kalyanak Mahotsav.

He is President of Shri Jainender Gurukul, Shri Jainender High School and Shri Jainender

Public School all at Panchkula. Shri Mahavir Jain Public Scool Kurukshetra, Lord Mahavir Foundation and Shri Subhagya Wati Jain Charitable Trust. He is the former trustee of Sh. All India S.S.Jain Congress and also the former President Sh. All India S.S.Jain Congress (Youth Wing) and former senate member Guru Nanak Dev University Punjab.

A man of credibility, this great man has influence on thousands of children and other people for the betterment of their lives. **India is very proud of Mr. Hira Lal Jain.**

V.K. Sood

V.K. Sood Engineers and Contractors is the leading company, **building roads and railway bridges all over India.** Started in 1969 and rose to build bridges on Jamuna, Ganga, Sutluj, Bias, Parveda rivers and many more.

Vinod Kumar (V.K.) with the help of his two sons Puneet and Vaneet, built 64 major bridges on 120 km long Railway Lines in J&K, between Quazi Gund and Baramulla. He was born in Ludhiana and married to Varsha. He also produced films Time Pass, Ghana Eak Rayke and Mahak Pyar Ki.

V.K. is the past President of Lion's Club of Panchkula and Ferozpur, ex-council man of Panchkula.

He is also the Chairman of Oscar's Institute of Art and Research, T.V. Channel ABTAK, Sood Sabha, Punjabi Bhaichara Mahasabha, Panchkula and International Roll Ball Federation.

V.K. is also the members of many Educational Trusts. He has organized many Cultural Functions in Schools.

These Indian personalities and their dedications are part of the Indian culture.

●

Chapter 14

Bollywood and Television

Tom Cruise said that he would love to do an Indian movie. "There are many Hindi movies that come out every year but I do watch a few of them." Cruise said. In India, people are in love with movies which include dozens of songs and dances of top stars, the story between the songs of boy meets girl and lots of action.

Indian films are shown in American, Canadian and in British theaters on a more and more frequent basis. These theaters have become community foci for the South Asian communities around the world. Indians have found Bollywood films to be a great way of staying in touch with their culture.

RAJ KAPOOR was the son of well-known Indian actor Prithviraj Kapoor, who acted both in films and on stage. After apprenticing in the Bollywood production studios of the 1940's, at 24 years of age, Raj Kapoor produced, directed and acted in Aag, with his new company, RK Films.

Mumbai is the centre of Hindi films. The stars of Bollywood are very popular. Providing three to four hours of entertainment is the primary objective of Bollywood and it's a recipe done well. By the 1930s, the industry was producing over 200 films per annum.

The period from the late 1940s to the 1960s is regarded as the "Golden Age" of Hindi cinema. Some of the most famous Hindi films of all time were produced during this period. Examples include the **Raj Kapoor films Awaara and Shree 420.** These films expressed social themes mainly dealing with working-class urban life in India; Awaara presented the city as both a nightmare and a dream,

Successful actors at the time included Dev Anand, Dilip Kumar, Raj Kapoor and successful actresses

included Nargis, Meena Kumari, Nutan, Madhubala.

In the late 1970s, romance movies and action films starred actors like **Rajesh Khanna, Dharmendra, and Shashi Kapoor and actresses like Sharmila Tagore and Asha Parekh. Amitabh Bachchan,** the star known for his "angry young man" roles, rode the crest of this trend with actors like **Mithun Chakraborty and Anil Kapoor.**

Hum Aapke Hain Kaun and Dilwale Dulhania Le Jayenge, making stars out of a new generation of actors such as **Aamir Khan, Salman Khan and Shahrukh Khan and actresses such as Madhuri Dixit, Juhi Chawla and Kajol.**

In 1990's, the action and comedy films with stunt actor **Akshay Kumar** was gaining popularity for performing dangerous stunts in action films.

Some of the largest production houses, among them Yash Raj Films and Dharma Productions were the producers of new modern films.

PRITHVI RAJ KAPOOR was a pioneer of Indian theatre and of the Hindi film industry, who started his career as an actor, in the silent era of Hindi cinema. His famous movie includes Mughal E Azam, where he gave his most memorable performance as the Mughal emperor Akbar.

DILIP KUMAR is considered to be one of the greatest actors of Indian cinema. Starting his career in 1944, he has starred in some of the biggest commercially successful films from the late 1940s, 1950s, 1960s and 1980s. His performances have been regarded as the epitome of emoting in Indian Cinema. One of his all time famous movie is Mughal-E-Azam where he gave a stellar performance as Prince Salim.

MADHUBALA—The most beautiful artist to ever grace the Indian screen, Madhubala rose from humble beginnings to become the most captivating star India has ever produced. Madhubala was born Mumtaz Jehan Begum on Valentine's Day 1933, in a poor, conservative family of Pathan Muslims in Delhi.

GURU DUTT—Kaagaz Ke Phool considered to be a man ahead of his time, Guru Dutt was one of the greatest icons of commercial Indian cinema. Although he made less than 50 films during his lifetime, they are believed to be the best to come from Bollywood's Golden Age, known both for their ability to reach out to the common man and for their artistic and lyrical content.

NARGIS—One of her best-known roles was that of Radha in the Academy Award-nomi-nated Mother India (1957), a performance that won her Best Actress trophy at the Filmfare Awards.

DHARMENDER—His most successful pairing was with Hema Malini, who went on to become his future wife. The couple played together in a large number of films, including Seeta Aur Geeta and Sholay. **In 1997, he received**

the Filmfare Lifetime Achieve-ment Award for his contribution to Hindi cinema.

SHAMMI KAPOOR received the Filmfare Best Actor Award in 1968. He made his Hindi Film debut in 1953 and went on to deliver hits like Junglee, Kashmir Ki Kali, An Evening in Paris and many more.

AMITABH BACHCHAN is the trademark deep baritone voice, the tall, brooding persona, and intense eyes, made Amitabh Bachchan the ideal "Angry Young Man" in the 1975-84. The son of the late poet Harivansh Rai Bachchan and Teji Bachchan, he was born in Allahabad in Uttar Pradesh.

WAHEEDA REHMAAN combined the classic Tamil-Islamic beauty, talent and a truly transcendent appeal that ranked her among the pantheon of Bollywood's elite actresses. And few could dance better than she could!

AISHWARYA RAI was the winner of the Miss World pageant of 1994. She received the Filfare Best Actress awards for her leading roles in Sanjay Leela Bhansali's 1999 melodrama Hum Dil De Chuke Sanam and the 2002 period film Devdas.

AKSHAY KUMAR is an Indian actor, producer and martial artist, who have performed in more than 100 films. **He has been nominated for Filmfare award many times and won it two times. He was awarded an Honorary Doctorate degree by a university in Canada.**

Television in India is a huge industry which has many programs in different languages. The small screen has produced many celebrities, some even attaining national fame. More than 50% of all Indian households own a television. There are over 500 TV channels in India and the cable industry is the third largest in the world. According to Pioneer Investcorp, the Indian cable industry is worth more than Rs 24,000 cr. ($4 Billion).

India's first soap opera, Hum Log, which concluded with 154 episodes, was the longest running serial in the history of Indian television at the time it ended. Every episode was about 25 minutes long, and the last episode was about 55 minutes.

The most common languages in which Indian serials are made are: Hindi, Punjabi, Marathi, Gujarati, Bengali, Tamil, Kannada, Telugu and Malayalam.

Satyamev Jayate is a show about interacting with the common man of India, deliberating with them the issues connected with the live issues in India.

Hindi soap operas have gained popularity all over the world. They are also aired in USA and Canada.

Indian Films and Television reflect the culture of India.

●

Chapter 15

Jeevan Prabhat

(Orphanage with a difference)

There was a deadly earthquake in Gujarat on 26th January 2001 where thousands of people died, leaving many children as orphans. There is a temple of Arya Samaj in Gandhidham, Gujarat where most dedicated people had spent their valuable time for the well being of their community. The authorities brought an infant to this Arya Samaj, whose parents died in that earthquake,

A young high ranking bank official, Acharya Vachonidhi, was one of those incredible community workers attached with this Arya Samaj. At that time

Mr. Vachonidhi was about 40 years old, he untiringly, helped the victims of this earthquake, day and night; he pulled many victims of this earthquake.

Another, internationally renowned person, Girish Khosla from USA, was visiting India and heard about this earthquake. He quickly went there to help the victims.

From one orphan infant of the earthquake of 2001, at Arya Samaj, Gandhidham it became 40-50 orphans in no time. The dedicated people of the Samaj took care of them physically, emotionally and financially. But the space was getting smaller and smaller as more children kept coming to this Arya Samaj.

With the help of the government and private donations, Arya Samaj built the beautiful facilities on 4 acres of land. This spotless place has marble/granite flooring. The entrance hall has a dome ceiling with Vedic teachings engraved on it. With open concept having garden in the middle, with beautiful flowers and nicely hedged fences of different shapes, all the buildings around makes this campus a very attractive place.

I first visited Jeevan Prabhat in January of 2012 for only 2 days. I liked the way about 200 children were being brought up like upper middle class children. I liked it so much that I came back again in January of 2013. This time I stayed there for more than 3 weeks and interacted with children to the great extent. There were about 200 children and staff members at the Campus.

The children got up at 5 in the morning and did prayers. I could hear them in my room which was on first floor of the main building. I was so happy to hear early morning prayers which I have not heard for more than

forty years of living in Canada. That reminded me of the stories we read in our childhood, about our great spiritual leaders' upbringing in this kind of atmosphere. I was so tempted that I would go downstairs and join them for the prayers.

The children then would go to their rooms and got ready to go to school. There are two, 3 storied wings, one for boys and other for girls. Each room has faculty for 2

to 4 children, depending upon the age. I have seen a one year old boy to a third year university student living at this campus. This one year old boy, like any other kid, wandered around the garden and other places, is the darling of every one. From staff to the other older children, they all wanted to play with him. I think this child would not have received the same kind of love and tender care at his own home. Each of these three storied wings have their own supervisors and then each floor has a senior child in-charge and responsible for the behavior of others in that area. These wings are locked at 9 pm from inside by the supervisor for the safety reason. The whole facility has high wall boundary and has security 24 hours a day. Nobody can come and leave the facilities without notifying the management. **The administration has strict rules and followed right to the letter. I noticed one day, a staff member neglected small part of his duty and next he was given strict warning by the management.**

There were grown up teenagers, boys and girls, but I was impressed to see the skill, how they handle dozens of them. Mr. Vachonidhi, the person incharge of the entire operation, told me that they never had any embarrassing situation. It is almost unbelievable, as we all know how difficult it is to handle our own 1-2 teenager children, let alone dozens of them. I think God is helping them.

Eating Breakfast

The children then got ready, at 6.30 to eat breakfast. There is a big hall on the main floor where more than 200

children can sit on the mats spread on the floor. There were several long rows where boys and girls sat in their own age groups. The food is cooked fresh every day by staff members in a kitchen with modern appliances. **Every day they make their own whole wheat floor in the kitchen with a small machine. The large gas stoves, steel fridges and steel counter tops and other facilities were no different than I have seen in America. There were 3-4 full-time cooks who prepare fresh breakfast, lunch and dinner for children in this very clean and modern kitchen.**

Cleanliness is the motto of this institution, it was

spotless everywhere. I did not notice any piece of paper or other mess anywhere at the Campus. The children are taught not to throw the garbage outside the bins and not to waste food. I think if all the people of India learn from this facility and from these children, it will be the cleanest country in the world and the people will be healthy and prosperous.

This place has its own facilities where they keep 30-40 cows to get fresh milk for the children. I used to visit this place, behind the main building, and watched how they were getting milk from these cows. Some of the senior children were helping workers. They also have their own small garden for fresh vegetables. They serve only vegetarian food to the children.

In the dining hall, there is hand washing facility. **Every child is required to wash hands before eating food. It was funny to see the younger children, trying to reach the taps by raising their feet.** It is strictly watched by the senior children. I noticed some children being lightly tapped on their shoulders for not properly washing their hands. I found out later, that the children were very healthy there. I believe, the proper hand washing is one of the major reasons for the children to be in good health.

Before the children come inside for eating, they stood in line outside the hall, in their age groups, the youngest and the girls being the first ones. There were no fights or arguments, senior children guided them at every step. I noticed the smile on their faces all the time. I found them to be very happy children. After washing hands, I noticed that they got their plates and stood in line to receive food being served by the senior children. They picked up a glass of milk and sat on the mats in rows. There were some senior children who supervised, while children ate food. All this was done very peacefully within 30-40 minutes. **After eating, children put out the plates, cups at proper places, washed their hands, picked up their school bags and went to schools in very modern yellow school buses.**

As they came near the gate to go on the buses, enrolment and counting was taken for each child and same thing was done on their return. They got in line to climb the buses in a very civilized manner, giggling, laughing like very happy children. You can't be happier than watching these kids in the morning. That used to make my day and I could not wait to see them in the evening. After seeing them off, I would get ready in my room on the first floor of the main building.

The guest room, where I stayed was like a suite in a 4-5 star hotel with attached bathroom with hot and cold water, colour TV, big closet, all carpeted with modern furniture with Internet facilities and much more. I felt like staying there forever, it was so comfortable. I used to have fresh breakfast in the beautiful garden every day.

The children came back from school about 1 pm. They were sent to regular schools where the tuition fee was paid for each child by the institution. The dress code was in force, so all these children had to dress up accordingly. The children were served fresh lunch, similar way. The children had their own time till about 3 pm when, afternoon classes would start to enhance their education. There are several classrooms on the first floor where dedicated teachers help children in their home work and teach new things also. **There was also a computer room with 15 new computers. This process lasted till about 5.30 pm when the children were free to play and do their own things.**

There is a beautiful park built on 2 acres of land at the campus. This park is beautifully landscaped with many kinds of flowers, nice and trimmed attractive hedges and trees. In the center, a large stage with canopy

and granite flooring is built for the important functions. The whole area is secured with wall boundary, high steel gates and by caretakers. This park is probably better than 90% of the parks I have seen in America.

This is where these beautiful children spend their time and play games. I noticed some instructors teaching them playing cricket, basketball, volleyball and other games. The girls were playing their own games, some sitting in groups talking, laughing and running just like normal kids. They were very happy there. They came back to their rooms at about 7 and then got ready for dinner. After the dinner, again there were prayers, after which it was TV time until 9 pm, at which time they went to bed. I noticed their big laughs watching TV. I believe this TV time is one of their most enjoyable time of the day.

There are many other facilities at the campus like music room with all kinds of instruments, piano room, library and other facilities. There is a large conference room where 300-400 people can sit. There are many functions, conferences and motivational speakers do their programs for the children. I attended one of those functions where a learned teacher gave them the advice on good living. This also is the place where the children do their act and drama. I attended one of these events and was impressed with their talent. Sunday is completely a free day, except that the older children go to the prayers at the Arya Samaj. I was impressed with the dedication of the President, Purshotam Patel and the treasurer, Guru Dutt Sharma.

Every year, children go to trips including Delhi, where one time they met Prime Minister and the President of India. They have also been to Mumbai, Udaipur, Haridwar, Rishikesh, Mansoori etc. Many people from various parts of India, America, Canada and other parts of the world support this magnificent institution which is the brain child of Girish Khosla and Vachonidhi Acharya.

I can visualize 200 some good productive, disciplined citizens coming out of Jeevan Prabhat and set an example for many. These children will help keeping the country clean. I had very good experience with them about cleaning, during my stay. The interiors of these facilities were very clean but the outside streets needed lot of care. During my first morning of 3 weeks stay, I got up early in the morning grabbed couple of small plastic bags to clean outside streets. I spent nearly an hour picking up plastic bags, candy wraps, plastic cups, newspaper pieces etc. My small bags were full, so I came inside the premises and gave those trash bags to the security guard standing at the gate to pile with the other trash as I did not know where the proper place was to dispose it off.

I was determined to make outside as clean as inside. It was like two different worlds. It is happening all over India where people keep inside of their homes neat and clean but the outside is dirty. I had heard a lot of it from the media and friends here in USA and Canada. I found Indian people living in India are much more intelligent than ones who lived abroad. I was even more astonished about super smart kids living in India. Even the children living in slum areas, were equally smart and knowledgeable, like the rest of the world.

We started a mission cleaning the streets of India. In my view, where intelligent people live, things can change quickly for the better and India is one of those places. It is a matter of explaining and brings the awareness among the people. The major difference is to throw trash in garbage bins instead of on the road. Like many other improvements, mobile phones, colour TVs, Highways, Metro, computers etc. in India, the cleanliness is next in line. The new generation is more organized and is determined to bring the changes.

With this in mind, early next morning I went outside to pick up trash in those garbage bags. I filled up one large bag and again, gave to the security guard to trash it. By the same evening, the management told me that all the students wanted to go with me to pick up the trash from the streets, outside the campus. I guess the security guard told them about my activities of last two days and they all got motivated. I was very happy. This was the last thing I ever expected. My vision of clean India was in the horizon, which is my dream. Next day, children made handwritten banners, got a drum and a portable microphone. I already had large plastic garbage bags bought earlier and bought some iron raking shovels that day and there we went on the streets to pick up trash. This was their play time but they wanted to go with me to clean the streets. I knew then that we have taken one big step to clean India. Within three days, from one person to about 200 children, staff, management to CEO, all voluntarily joined me to clean their area.

We did few more cleanings during my stay with them. One day we all decided to go to do the cleaning in the main market. Lot more people joined the children; we had green dresses for youngsters to symbolize the importance of greenery.

Management of Arya Samaj, Gandhidham, Jeevan Prabhat and local business people joined us. There was a big dump truck following us to store the trash being picked by the children and others. These were happy days of my life. I had been in touch with the management after my return and being told that the children are keeping the tradition of cleaning outside their place. On my last day, after about three weeks stay, I had a seminar with the children about hygienic values and did few demos including how to effectively wash hands with soap five times a day, coughing on elbows instead of in hands, holding spoons from stem etc. I hope, I made some dent in their lives. I am looking forward to meet these children again very soon.

Swami Dayanand Saraswati founded the Arya Samaj on 10th April 1875 with the aim of promoting the spiritual, social and physical well being of mankind. Although Arya Samaj is universal in character, its principal field of activity has been the Hindu Society.

It is Arya Samaj that revolutionized the religious thoughts and ideas of Hindus. Arya Samaj taught people to think rationally and intelligently before accepting or acceding to any religious dogma. It shed a new light on the ignorance, blind faith, superstitious beliefs, customs and beliefs which had polluted the Hindu mind and society. The Principles of Arya Samaj were enunciated to be conducive to our well being in every sphere of life. Arya Samaj is a movement not merely concerned with worship, prayer and Vedic philosophy but its teachings embrace all aspects of life and living. Arya Samaj's activity permeates the social, political, economic, commercial, educational and universal concerns. Arya Samaj is a society of noble men and women.

Arya Samaj believes in the existence and worship of one God only. It also believes in the trinity of God, Soul and Matter, each of them being endowed with its own characteristics. It believes that God can be realized through the combination of deed, knowledge and devotion. Arya Samaj propagates that one should not be contented with one's own well being but consider the well being of others as one's own well being. Arya Samaj lays great emphasis on an individual's life. It believes that in today's world immorality, greed, bribery, deceit, violence and dishonesty is rife. To contain and overcome these evils, a virtuous conduct and moral life should be every one's forte. It believes in, and encourages the performance of the sixteen "Sanskaras". It also believes in the four definite stages that will lead to a fuller development of an individual physically, mentally and spiritually. These are (1) Brahmacharya, (2) Grihasta, (3) Vanaprastha and (4) Sanyas ashrams.

Arya Samaj has all along campaigned for the

freedom of thought. It prides itself in reviving the Vedas and encourages everyone irrespective of caste, creed or sex to read them. Arya Samaj denounces the malpractice of blind faith and strongly believes in the equality of every one in social, educational and political attainment. This includes women as well. It believes in widow remarriage but denounces child marriage and dowry system. Arya Samaj repudiates the caste system, is against meaningless post death customs and rituals, and is against untouchability. It encourages "Shuddhi" movement and education and equal rights for women. Swami Dayanand and other prominent Arya Samajists fought for the independence of India. Arya Samaj has always campaigned for Hindi to be the national language of India.

Arya Samaj performs its duty with sincerity and total devotion. Its principles are in conformity with the laws of nature and science. Arya Samaj prides in the contribution, dedication and total devotion of its members wherever they are in the world, to its cause and spread of Vedic knowledge and culture. Arya Samaj has contributed and still continues to contribute for the maintenance of global peace, harmony and universal brotherhood.

Reforms by Swami Dayanand Saraswati

Swami Dayanand Saraswati carried out reforms in the fields of Religion, Social and Politics.

Religious Reforms: Swamiji did not intend to start a new religious order. He stressed that he wanted to reveal all that is in the Vedas. According to the Vedas there is only one God who is Omnipresent, Unborn, and Formless. He eradicated witchcraft, blind faith and rigid practices. He spoke against idol worship. He stressed the importance of the Vedic religion. He strongly protested against the practice of animal sacrifice.

Political Reforms: Swami Dayanand urged Indians to fight for their independence from the foreign yoke. He said that only free nations can make progress. This call was made before the creation of any political party in India. He was not afraid of facing prosecution for making such statements. He believed it was birth right of every one to be free and have access to true education. Many other revolutionaries like Lala Lajpat Rai, Sardar Bhagat Singh, Chandra Sekhar Azad and Ram Prasad Bismil were all Arya Samajists. The historians should remember the contributions of Swami Dayanand Saraswati in the struggle for independence of India.

Social Reforms : Swamiji brought about several social reforms. He protested against the practice of child marriage, advocated widow remarriage, eradicated the evil of untouchability, and protested against the caste system but supported the theory of four classes—Brahmin, Kshatriya, Vaisya, and Shudra on the basis of their aptitude and not related to their birth. He established equality between men and women and encouraged women to read and write and become literate. He planned the Gurukul System of education based on the teachings of the Vedas. He also undertook "Shuddhi" of those Hindus who due to some reason had been misled to adopt other religion.

The sixth principle of Arya Samaj states that, "the

primary aim of the Arya Samaj is to do good for all, that is, to promote physical, spiritual and social well-being."

Many of the evils which Maharishi Dayanand Saraswati had eradicated have once again engulfed the Hindu Society. There is a need to carry out various reforms once again. There is a need to have many more people with the qualities of Swami Dayanand Saraswati to undertake these tasks. Arya Samaj too can play an important role to undertake various reforms.

What some prominent persons said about Swami Dayanand Saraswati:

"As I regard the figure of this formidable artisan in God's workshop, images crowd on me which are all of battle and work, conquest and triumphant labour. Here, I say to myself, was a very soldier of light, a warrior in God's world, a sculptor of man and institutions, a bold and rugged victor of the difficulties, which matter presents to spirit. And the whole sums itself up to me in a powerful impression of spiritual practicality. The combination of these two words, usually so divorced from each other in our conceptions, seems to me the very definition of Dayanand." *—Sri Aurobindo*

"I offer my homage of veneration to Swami Dayanand, the great path maker in northern India, who through bewildering tangles of creed and practices, the dense undergrowth of the degenerate days of our country, cleared a straight path that was meant to lead the Hindus to a simple and rational life of devotion to God and service for man." *—Rabindra Nath Tagore*

"By declaring that everyone, including women and non-Brahmins had the right to study the Vedas and by rendering them into Hindi, the language of the common people, both of which were considered a sacrilege, Dayanand brought about a revolution which by one masterstroke shattered the shackles, which Hindus had borne for centuries." *—Lala Lajpat Rai*

"Swami Dayananda Saraswati is certainly one of the most powerful personalities who has shaped modern India and is responsible for its moral regeneration and religious revival". *—Subhas Chandra Bose*

"A master spirit has passed away from India. Pandit Dayanand Saraswati is gone; the irrepressible, energetic Reformer, ...whose might voice and passionate eloquence for the last few years raised thousands of people in India from lethargic indifference and stupor into active patriotism, is no more." *—Colonel H.S. Olcot*

President, Theosophical Society

"Whatever one may think of the correctness or other-wise of Swami Dayanand's interpretation of many Vedic passages, one cannot withhold one's admiration for a man whose work, perhaps more than that of any other individual, has helped to make India conscious of itself as unity with some distinctive contribution to make to the culture of the world as a whole."

—Dr. R.L. Turner

Haverbrack Bishop's Storford

"I have observed, during my travels in India, the effects of Swami Dayanand Saraswati's influence in earnest efforts to vitalise life in India with the Vedic ideal, which for thirty years had been a fundamental influence in my own life and in that of Mrs. Cousins and for this much-needed service to India and the world; I offer our joint homage to his memory."

—*Dr. James H. Cousins,* D. Litt.

The primary aim of the religions in India is to do good for all, that is, to promote physical, spiritual and social well-being, which are part of the Indian culture.

●

Chapter 16

$20 Billion to $200 Billion

India has the potential of earning $200 Billion (Rs. 12 Lakh Crore) from the current earnings of about $20 Billion (Rs. 1.2 Lakh Crore) from foreign tourism. Few years ago, an advertisement of Taj Mahal, in a Canadian National newspaper, prompted me to search about the foreign tourists to the Taj Mahal and the other wonders of the world. I noticed, the number of tourists at Eiffel Tower were 10 times more than the number of foreign tourists at Taj Mahal.

While comparing with Eiffel Tower, I noticed that not only, there is a big structural difference between these two, but Taj Mahal also has a love story attached to it. **This love story, wrapped in the white marble, is the Taj Mahal.** It was built about 500 years ago. It is a beautiful piece of art and represents the Indian culture. It took about 20 years to build the Taj Mahal by about 20,000 people. This is much different from Eiffel Tower, a steel structure, which was built about 150 years ago.

I further started looking into the reasons, why such a beautiful monument receives a low number of foreign tourists. I talked to many Americans and Canadians and found out that everyone wants to see the Taj Mahal then, why aren't they coming? I was curious. When President

Clinton's daughter, Chelsea, visited the Taj at her younger age in 1995, she described it as her dream of fairy-tale palace of her childhood coming true. She further said "I see pictures of Taj Mahal and would dream I was a princess or whatever....."

Many Americans and Canadians want to see the Taj Mahal but are afraid of cleaning and hygienic conditions in India. My youngest daughter used to come to India with us when she was younger. She loved it so much and would say, "When I grow up and become a doctor, I will come to India every year and will help poor people". In 2010, she came to New Delhi to do shopping for her wedding. Next day she called me from there saying, "Dad never ask me to come here again, it is very dirty." I was shocked and very much concerned. I had not been to India for more than 10 years and did not realize the conditions were so bad there.

I was in Bangkok, visiting my friend, Kuljit, who told me that his son would not go to India to attend a wedding even for just 2 days, as he felt very uncomfortable there due to lack of cleanliness and lack of toilets. Another friend of Kuljit told me the same story that his children would not go to India.

This raised lot of questions in my mind that our children will miss the big part of this beautiful culture. An Indian ex-Member of Parliament of Canada told me that not only our children but, even many parents do not want to go back to India due to cleaning and hygienic conditions there.

Then I watched the movie, Slum Dog Millionaire in Canada. They showed the garbage all over in the slums of Mumbai. I was curious if India was that dirty. It was not like this a few years ago when I was in India last time; I wanted to see it myself in person. The reputation of cleanliness of India is bad. It is discouraging the tourists, and hurting the country economically, also. I wanted to do something about it.

I came to India in December of 2011 after 13 years. After visiting family and friends for a few days, I went to Mumbai to see Dharavi, the slum areas shown in the movie, Slum Dog Millionaire. This was a very large area with high density of small slum houses. I walked through the narrow streets noticing small business shops on both sides.

People were busy making products like, card board boxes, printing business cards and brochures, making shoes, toys, clothes and so on. There were many retail shops of clothing, food, tea vendors etc. I was surprised to see the number of mobile phone shops. Almost everybody had a mobile phone with him.

I found the main streets were dirty but inside streets were kept clean by the house owners on both sides of it. In a few open areas, I found some piles of

garbage but nothing like what they showed in this movie. I went to another slum area and spent more than 10 days there. Again I found a pile of garbage in one area, rest of the area was not that dirty. People had colour televisions, musical systems and lap tops. The children were so smart and had vast general knowledge about the surroundings and the world.

I could not believe the difference in what I saw in person and what I had seen in this movie. I already had plans to start a cleaning project in India. I wanted to see a clean India for the children and for the tourists to India without fear of getting sick.

I went to another slum area and made suggestions to clean up their area. In the beginning, they would not listen but I kept going there for 2-3 days. They were not interested in cleaning, saying that the area will get dirty again due to the habits of the people.

Finally, I met the Secretary of the Association of this area and showed him some pictures of the other areas where we had already done cleaning projects.

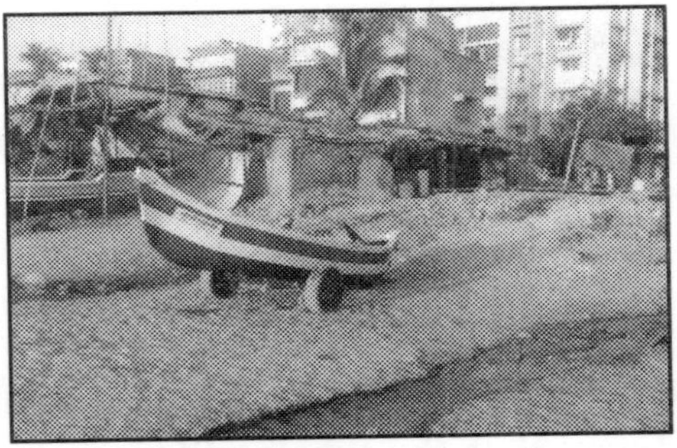

This convinced the Secretary and he promised to call a public meeting to discuss the issue. As I insisted that we should clean the area first, he agreed. We hired the trucks and cleaned most of the area. This was a smaller slum area of about 400-500 houses with about 1000 children. We implanted some trees and installed some benches. Later, I found out that people would sit outside and play music etc. at that clean area.

One day, we were traveling to another city in a car. I asked the driver to stop in a village. This village was near the city of Karnal. People there treated us with love and care. I explained them about my mission of cleaning. I told them that I liked to see this village really clean and to set up an example for others. In the beginning they did not believe; thought that I was some kind of politician. As my driver explained of my mission and that I had come from Canada, they started listening more carefully. I made some suggestions after walking through some areas. I offered them money to buy the material to improve the streets. They refused to take it but as I insisted, they took the money.

Few days later, I called their leader and was very happy to know that the whole village got motivated into cleaning. Two weeks later, I went to visit them again and took green barrels and green hats with me to give them. This time more than 70 people got together, about half of them were children. We discussed about the benefits of cleanliness. We also discussed the problems of drainage that the people were throwing trash in the open water drainage system and blocking it. At the end, they formed a committee to solve these problems.

One of the high school students told me that he would get all his school friends together and clean the village as there were lots of benefits of cleanliness. I was very happy to hear this from the youngsters, the awareness about the benefits of cleanliness. A place, a city or a country can only be cleaned by bringing the awareness among their people. No one person or a group can clean the area for ever.

Campaign in School

One day, a friend told me that making children aware of cleaning at a young age is the best way to go around. He told me that whatever he learned at his early age, he still follows it. This made a good sense to me. Earlier, we did cleaning in some areas, but when we went there again, it was not as clean as I left it earlier.

By this time, we had formed a few groups and I suggested them these ideas of teaching young children at schools. We did a small demo in a school in Ludhiana with about 70-80 children and showed them how to throw garbage in bins, how to effectively wash hands, how to do coughing in elbows, how to pick spoons from the handle and many more. That was my last day in Ludhiana during that trip.

Few days later, I called the CEO of that institution and was very happy from his response. He told me that he had 26,000 students under his organization and requested me to do similar demo for all his students. That day, I got convinced that India can be cleaned in 10-12 years.

In one of my trips, I came to visit an orphan's place called Jeevan Prabhat, at Gandhidham in Gujarat. This is amazing place housing about 200 children in a very neat and clean facility. The outside of these premises was very dirty. I stayed there for a few days. Next day, early in the morning, I got up and went outside on the street and found some empty plastic bags. I filled these bags with the trash and came inside the premises and gave to the security guard to dump it.

This place, Jeevan Prabhat, is secured with boundary wall and has 24 hours security. The same afternoon I went to the market and bought 40 large black garbage bags to collect the trash. Next day, early in the morning I

went outside again and filled out one garbage bag with trash and gave to the security guard again. In the evening, as I came back, I met the manager of this institution, who told me that all the children wanted to go out cleaning the streets with me. I guess the security guard told them about my morning's activities. I was very happy about their initiative. I suggested that I would get some banners and brochures printed, but the children wanted to make their own hand-written banners.

I bought some iron shovels. I already had a lot of garbage bags. The children made the banners. They collected a drum set and a portable microphone system. Three days later we were in the streets of Gandhdham with about 200 children, their staff and the management people including Acharya Vachonidhi, a very dedicated person who manages this and many other institutions. The children were beating the drums, repeating the slogans on the benefits of cleaning, others were picking up the trash, some of them were distributing the flyers which we prepared earlier, and others were talking to residents about the benefits of cleaning and so on.

It was an amazing scene like a shooting a film. All the kids wanted to do this cleaning. I did not ask

anyone to follow me. They all wanted to see their place a clean place, like all the Indians do. All was needed a little vehicle, an excuse, a way to do. Once they found that, it became a common theme, a purpose to be healthier in a clean place. We must have filled 30-40 large garbage bags that day. We repeated the same operation three more times in the same area.

Then the management suggested doing the cleaning in the core part of the city. One afternoon, they made the arrangement with Municipality to provide us with a big garbage truck to follow us in the market as the children paraded through the streets of the down town. We rented special green dresses for some small children, symbolizing the importance of green and clean environment. Lots of other people joined us to bring the awareness among the population.

Mission

About 6 million foreign tourists came to India in 2012 spending about $20 billion (Rs 1,20,000 cr.) according to The Times of India. This amount can be increased to $200 billion (Rs 12,00,000 cr.) in 10-12 years. The best way to achieve this goal is to encourage foreign tourists to come here in a large number. **According to the United Nations figures, tourism is the largest industry in the world and employs more people than any other industry. Countries with a large number of tourists have developed at a faster pace.**

Countries like France, USA, Spain and many others, receive more than 60 million tourists every year. The tourism has a lot of impact on the developments of these countries. India has even more potential, having such an amazing history and historical monuments. It can achieve the target of 60 million tourists in the next 10-12 years. This will create huge employment and will bring a lot of foreign money, resulting in strengthening in our currency and bringing prestige to the country, which, once it had. Indian currency was at par with the dollar in 1947.

During last many years, I found out from some foreigners about, what was discouraging them to visit India. Most people in America and Canada want to visit India and especially to see the Taj Mahal. Indian Culture is one of the oldest cultures in the world and foreigners are fascinated about it. I was visiting a family where a young Canadian couple was also present. They were so anxious about India and wanted to visit it, but were afraid of getting sick there. Another close friend of mine, Eric (retired bank manager), told me that he will not visit India as he was afraid of diseases there. Eric is retired now and has travelled many parts of the world. There are more than 50 million retirees in America and Canada and their main purpose of life is to see the world. They have time and money to spend.

George (PhD), about 40 years old, came to India in 2013. Earlier, his mother would not let him go. She told me that she was afraid that George would get sick in India. George took a lot of medicines with him. George spent 3-4 weeks in India, I met him on his return and he was fine. He did not get sick. But the perception of getting sick in the people's mind is there. We need to remove this by cleaning our country. On top of it, it is healthier for our children.

As I have noticed, during last three years, everyone in India wants to see, clean surroundings and streets. But, not many people are willing to take initiative to do it. "It is not my job", most of them told me. Further, they told me, "How one person can make a difference." I kept telling them my story of starting with one person to nearly 200 in one school alone. This can be done by anyone, in my opinion. I found the youngsters (15-40) are more keen and excited for this idea of cleaning, than the later generation.

As it is well known, that the Indians are one of the most intelligent people in the world, we can reach our target of 60 million tourists a year. I suggest the following to reach our target of generating $200 billion a year from the tourism:

1. **We should start teaching cleaning and hygienic values to the school children at an early age.** I have tried to clean some area in 3 different cities but it was not kept as clean afterwards, although I noticed some improvements. It looks that the people have these habits for long time and it is hard to change them, but the habits of the youngsters can be changed. Now, we have started doing this campaign in schools.

Recently, we did a demo on cleaning and hygienic values in a school with about 700 students and teachers. The Principal and the Management got so impressed that they are now planning to have a class, once a week, from next session just for the purpose of teaching the cleaning and hygienic values to the children.

This can be done in every school of India. Today's child of 5-15 will be old enough in 10 years to make a dent in changing habits. This age group will be in a large number in a few years and will a have significant impact on parents, grandparents and others to change their old habits also.

2. **Each street should have a group of volunteers. Each District can be divided into groups, each group consisting of a population of 10,000 people.** Average District in India has 2 million people, so there could be 200 group leaders in it. Each group leader should have volunteers for each street. Everybody wants to see his street clean, but somebody needs to take the lead. It is that group leader, who has passion for cleanliness, can make the difference. It is the responsibility of the people, not of the government to keep the streets clean. The government should provide the facility to take the trash away from the streets to the proper dumping places.

3. **All sides of the highways need to be cleaned.** In America, most cities do the cleaning campaign every 3-6 months, where 2,000-3,000 volunteers get together and pick up trash on the sides of the roads and highways. We should form groups of volunteers to clean the highways.

4. **Areas around the railway lines need to be cleaned.** I travelled between Delhi and Agra and also some other areas by train and noticed trash all over. All the railway employees and passengers should keep the railway sites clean.

5. **India needs to build public pay-washrooms in the commercial areas of every city and on the highways. I believe India needs 120,000 such washrooms from the tourist's point of view.** These washrooms will also provide bath and cold drinking water facilities for the public. These pay-washrooms, needed to be operated on entrepreneurship principles on the streets of the markets, where the operator owns this business and charges certain fees for the usage and make profit for him. Cleaner the place, more money he will be able to make. He should also be required to keep clean a 500 yard area of each side of the street. Each 1000 yard of these streets, should have a pay-washroom. These pay washrooms should also be built at every 50 kilometer of the highways. These washrooms can provide employment to 500,000-600,000 people. This way the market streets and highways will be kept clean. These washrooms will be useful to both the local people and the tourists. If the governments provide the land and utilities, a small washroom can be built for $9,000-10,000 (Rs 500,000-600,000).

6. **Obtaining a Visa for India, from a foreign country, has been a discouragement for tourists, NRIs and business people.** Recently, I was in Toronto, in one of Indian Visa offices to obtain a visa, it was a mess there. There were about 200 people and it was a wait of 5-6 hours just to submit the application. There were many Canadians, waiting and got discouraged from the lengthy process. After 5 p.m., there were still 40-50 people waiting for their turn and the officials tried to close the office. But on people's objection, they started processing

the applications again. One Canadian showed me the poster on the wall there saying, "Incredible India", he laughed and said, yes it is really incredible with this type of bureaucracy here. The government of India is moving at a very slow speed to improve these small things besides the other difficulties which foreigners face in India. Some Canadians were saying, that for China, one can apply in the morning and receive Visa, the same afternoon.

7. **Cashing the traveller's cheques or even to cash the foreign currency is very difficult in India.** Banks close these facilities by 3 or 4 pm. Besides this, currency exchange discount is too high. I have seen as much as 10% discount between buying and selling rates. We should learn these from Bangkok, where you can get currency exchanged at very low discount and during most of the business hours. They also cash the traveller's cheques immediately, vs. many days in India.

There are so many other ways we can encourage foreign tourists to come to India. The time is now. It is the efforts of both the government and the public. I believe, until people help and co-operate, this target cannot be achieved.

A clean India will be good for the culture and for the economy of the country.

●

Conclusion

The culture of each country is different from that of the other. Each country can be proud of its culture. Every country has something special to be emulated by others. America is considered to be the most developed and the richest country in the world. India, on the other hand, is still a developing country and lags behind America in terms of materialistic values. However, materialism is not only means to give happiness and peace.

Money and Power did not always make people happier. History is witness from Roman Empire to Napoleon and Hitler. A mother, in an Indian movie, said to the friend of her son, "strongest man does not win; it is the humanity and the nobleness which wins". She further said, "Hitler was a strong man, but he did not win." This friend wanted to take revenge on the killers of her son.

Taking care of others is humanity; this is what the Indian culture is all about. Whether it is the parents, sacrificing for the well being of their children or for children to take care of their parents after retirement. Both are winners and the tradition keeps going. I just met a waiter, Narayan, in a restaurant, who's grown up son, was getting education in another city. I found Narayan, always smiling and happy. One day he told me that he was spending two thirds of his earnings for his son's education. He said that his son's education was more important to him than anything else in his life, as his son will become a professional and a happy person thereafter.

Another person, Brij, told me that he was buying a house for his second son. He could have gone on vacation, enjoyed his money, but his priority was to establish his children and to see them happy. It is different with Americans, where sacrificing for others is not very common. In America, 50% children are fatherless (either unwed mothers or divorced parents). I heard many commentators on US televisions saying that the lack of father's role in the child's life is the reason for increase in crimes in America. There are 40 times (per capita) more people in Jails in America than in India. Divorce is one big reason for many of the problems in America. I believe this is something, the Americans can learn from the Indians.

There is a big difference in early age education between the American schools and the Indian schools. All the multiplication tables are taught in the Indian schools, three years ahead of the American schools. Further, due to the method of teaching, Indian kids remember these even at later stage of their life, but most Americans don't.

In a recent world survey on reading, India came on top in "hours of reading per week" being, 10 hours compared to 5 hours in America, 6 hours in Australia (Times of India).

An American, Friya, who had worked very hard in an ICU unit in a Los Angeles Hospital, got frustrated from the hard work, overtimes and from her stressful life. She quit her high paying job and came to India about 25 years ago. Now she wants to spend rest of her life in India. She loves the culture and the way of life in India. She is very happy and keeps herself busy with her activities, which she could not have done otherwise. Dr. Bhushan Sood of Panchkula, is a close contact of Friya, who helped and guided her to achieve a happy life in India. Dr. Sood is very active in helping the Indian as well as the Canadian society. He spends a great amount of time in both countries.

In March of 2014, Governor General of Canada, Mr. David Johnston visited India. In an interview with Indrani Bagchi of The Times of India he stated, "I am very thrilled to be in India." He further said, "This time, my wife has come with me. On another visit, I want to bring some of my 10 grandchildren along."

India is a great country and has the best culture in the world.

●●

About the Author

The author was born in Ludhiana in 1947. He got his education in India and in USA. He has been living in Canada for the last 40 years and started many businesses.

Being an Indian born and constantly worried about the problems people face here, he wrote an article which was published in The Times of India on January 9,1995. In this article he drew the attention about the traffic accidents and improper care of the wounded in India. He made many suggestions to improve the ways of handling such a situation. The author was very happy to know that many of those suggestions were implemented later in the years to come.

By instinct, the author has been a fighter against a wrongful act. Upon arrival in Canada, the author faced many problems and fought against them. In 1979, a policeman was disciplined in Canada upon his complaint for issuing a wrongful traffic violation ticket. Again in 2003, another policeman issued a wrongful violation ticket against the author. Upon his complaint and lengthy investigation (about 3 years long), the policeman was punished with suspensions, a record was made against him and he was sent for further training etc. Further, the policeman apologized in writing. This resulted in escalation of police behavior against the author. Within months, more wrongful violation tickets and criminal charges were laid against the author to harass him.

Even though the author is not a lawyer, he fought all these cases by obtaining knowledge from the law libraries and won all of them. Then he sued the police, public prosecutors and others (altogether 22 persons) for millions of dollars in two different fillings, in the Canadian civilian courts for malicious prosecution and conspiracy. Fighting with seven lawyers and going through the cumbersome process of the court process for six years, the author succeeded in forcing the defendants to settle the cases outside the court on his terms.

In 2005, he filed a case against Ford Motor Company and two other associated companies (for a defected vehicle), who were represented by three lawyers. After three years of fighting in the court, the settlement was made in author's favor. This time also, he fought the case by himself.

There were two other civil cases represented by the Canadian lawyers, again he won all of them.

Author started an Indian-Canadian Business and Professional's Association in Canada in 1980 which was, perhaps, the first association of it's kind in Canada. Further, the author formed many other social organizations in USA and in Canada.

In 2011, author came to India after 13 years with the mission of cleaning the country. To pursue his goals, he started the campaign in many cities of India. Eventually, the goal is to reach all the Districts (About 640) of India and make them clean and green for the sake of the health of the children and for the economy of the country.

A large amount of funds, raised from the sale of this book, will be used for this purpose.

Acknowledgement

This book is the result of sincere and hard work of many people. I like to especially thank Deepak Bhatt for his dedication and hard work. He constantly worked with me for nearly two years to search and write this book. I like to thank Acharya Vachonidhi and Arya Samaj Gandhidham for inspiring me and providing facilities in writing this book till the last minute of printing this book.

Thanks to Dr Balvir Acharya who has provided material on Yoga and Hinduism and also introducing to many people who have helped me in writing this book in many ways.

Dr. S. K. Maini has been my mentor and guide on many topics which I have discussed with him very often. His book, Madan Mohan Malaviya, was instrumental in writing about Malaviyaji in this book Our family relations go back nearly one hundred years with Dr. Maini's family. I sincerely, like to thank him for all the help and guidance.

My school friend, Satinder Mahajan has encouraged me and introduced to many people including Mr. Hira Lal Jain of Ludhiana who helped me in writing this book.

My brother, V.K. Sood, stood by me all the way through and provided his staff whenever I needed for writing this book, I am very thankful to him.

Thanks to Dr. Sudhi Kant Bhardwaj and K. Chandan for helping me in many way.

I am thankful to Ramesh Malhotra for helping in printing this book.

My childhood friend, C.K. Maini, constantly provided material and inspiration to me to write this book until his death in 2012. I talked to him almost every day from Canada to Delhi for 2-3 years before he left this world. We played and went to school together since the age of 4. I miss him every day. This book is dedicated to him.

Further, thanks to my family and all the people who have helped and inspired me to write this book.

My special thanks to all the people of India, who have taught me many things, in more than one way, which I could never have learned from any other community or source. I am deeply obligated.

●●